James and the Children

BY ELI SIEGEL

Hot Afternoons Have Been in Montana: Poems

The Aesthetic Method in Self-Conflict

Is Beauty the Making One of Opposites?

Art As Life

Psychiatry, Economics, Aesthetics

Shakespeare's Hamlet: Revisited

Williams' Poetry Talked About by Eli Siegel and William Carlos Williams Present & Talking: 1952

JAMES AND
THE CHILDREN

A CONSIDERATION OF HENRY JAMES'S
THE TURN OF THE SCREW

BY ELI SIEGEL

Edited by Martha Baird

DEFINITION PRESS   New York

Library of Congress Catalog Card Number 67-31121

Second Printing, 1969

Printed in the United States of America

Contents

Foreword, 1967

Evil has certainly continued since James wrote his *Turn of the Screw* in the late 1890's. So it is as necessary as ever to ask what evil is.

One gets the feeling that evil in Miles and Flora has to do with their separation from the feelings of others. The present-day alienation, so dismally popular, is an insufficient interest in feeling existing elsewhere than in oneself.

And since Flora and Miles, other children have been born. Each has had the tendency and likelihood to see himself or herself as too disjoined from what else was. We are much but what we are not is much, too.

Has this to do with 1914 and 1939 and 1967 and the suffering then? Have the Somme, Stalingrad, Dakto to do with the way children are born and how they are encouraged to be? or let to be?

Every person now demonstrated against was once untalkative, unappointed, unshaped. Within every person, though, was a likelihood. And there are two great likelihoods in the world: good and evil.

Miles and Flora do something to truth, to suit themselves. When you think you have the right to do something to truth, the right goes on to include doing things, to suit yourself, with people.

It happens that James's propaganda is his technique. His technique is an asking of what is within a person, not seen, and the asking some more, and the asking in as many ways as mind itself may ask for. His propaganda is that if we are not interested in the feelings of others, in the feelings walking about as people walk, sitting as people sit, lying down as people lie down—we may be either deceived by them or be cruel to them.

From evil seen and unseen in man, beginning where he begins, we have the fall of Madrid.

James makes the unseen less unseen. Here he is with St. Francis, William Godwin, Christ, John Brown, William Cobbett, Jane Addams.

In words added as Epilogue, technique as kind to man is talked of.

ELI SIEGEL

December 1967

Editor's Introduction

In 1953, Eli Siegel gave a series of lectures on Henry James which culminated in an explanation of *The Turn of the Screw,* James's famous and baffling short novel about two ghosts, two children, a governess and a housekeeper. Siegel, looking at the text closely and considering it in relation to James's other works, came to a conclusion at variance with a widely held interpretation of the story.

The question is, Is the governess good or bad? Is she to be accepted at face value, a James heroine in good standing, telling her story in the James style; or is she deluded, inventing the ghosts and attributing evil to the children which is really in herself? If the governess is bad, the credibility of the narrator is questioned, and the common sense of the ordinary reader who believes her— as he believes Robinson Crusoe—is challenged. One of Siegel's points is that many people have preferred this to thinking that real evil can be in pretty little children, aged about eight and ten. The story, he shows, brings up the question, What is evil, and when or where does it begin?

The Oxford Companion to American Literature by James D. Hart, published in 1941, is a reference work in good standing. Hart's article on *The Turn of the Screw* summarizes the story in accordance with a view of it

Siegel is opposing, a view first made popular by Edmund
Wilson in 1934. Wilson, influenced by the ideas of Freud,
presented the governess as bad and the children as
maligned and injured by her. Hart does not use the word
bad, he just says "neurotic." His account, however, while
supposed to be a factual description of the narrative, is
really an interpretation; for the "neurotic governess" is
an idea of later critics, it is not what Henry James himself anywhere says. But it has gotten to be part of our
culture, and both a play and an opera based on *The Turn
of the Screw* presented the governess and the children
in this way.

   The Turn of the Screw was published in 1898. I quote
the account given by Hart in the *Oxford Companion:*

> This mysterious tale of ghostly apparitions is recounted
> from the diary of a neurotic spinster who in her youth was
> a governess on a lonely British estate. Her unusually beau-
> tiful and precocious pupils, the children Miles and Flora,
> are subjected, she believes, respectively to the evil in-
> fluences of two ghosts: Peter Quint, once steward of the
> estate, and Miss Jessel, their former governess. The frus-
> trated new governess, infatuated by the children and par-
> ticularly by the boy, pits her will against that of the
> ghosts, for these specters, she believes, morally dominate
> the children and have an evil relationship with them. She
> justifies her belief by winning the housekeeper to her
> cause, although this kindly, simple woman never sees the
> apparitions. Fearing to report the untoward events to her
> employer, the children's uncle, for whom she entertains an
> unrealized and thwarted passion, the governess attempts
> to exorcise the malignant influences by directly challenging
> Flora, whose resultant fear is so great she cannot again
> face the governess. A similarly impassioned attack on Miles
> results in his death in the arms of the governess, who
> thought she was saving his life from a demon.

While having much currency, this idea of *The Turn of the Screw* has also been questioned—notably in an essay of 1948 by Robert Heilman, which Eli Siegel discusses, and likewise by Leon Edel.

In these talks, Siegel's manner of approaching the James story was a little like that of James himself. He didn't tackle it head-on, he circled round it. He began the series with a discussion of the novel in general, then he got to James, then to James's critical writings, information about his life, and quite a few of James's other stories and novels. Every now and then he'd make a comparison to *The Turn of the Screw,* showing a similarity or a difference. For example, in *What Maisie Knew,* published in 1897, one year before *The Turn of the Screw,* the heroine, Maisie, is a little girl. Showing the difference between Maisie and Flora in *The Turn of the Screw,* Siegel makes it clear that Henry James knew how to present a child who was lovable, charming, bright, and convincingly good if he wanted to.

It is not because Aesthetic Realism differs from Freud that Eli Siegel opposes the Edmund Wilson version of *The Turn of the Screw;* it is, as will be seen, because of what he finds in James.

Siegel's criticism is distinguished in three ways: its faithfulness to James's text, its logical coherence, and its originality. The highest originality is the manner in which literary criticism is at one with a way of seeing man, art, and the world itself. This is Aesthetic Realism.

Siegel's *Four Statements of Aesthetic Realism* are a description, in simple language, of the basic ideas of this philosophy:

1. Every person is always trying to put together opposites in himself.
2. Every person in order to respect himself has to see the world as beautiful or good or acceptable.
3. There is a disposition in every person to think he will be for himself by making less of the outside world.
4. All beauty is the making one of opposites, and the making one of opposites is what we are going after in ourselves.

These statements are constantly relevant to *The Turn of the Screw*, but it is the elaboration of point three in particular that explains the horror.

The Turn of the Screw is gripping, and carries with it an atmosphere of mystery and suspense hardly equalled in fiction. One does not know what is going on between the children and the ghosts: apparently all the ghosts do is appear and give looks; but the reader feels something dreadful is happening or about to happen. What it is, James never tells.

If you follow the Freudians and start saying the governess is imagining a homosexual relation between Miles and Quint, and some ghostly lesbianism between Flora and Miss Jessel—it takes on a ludicrous quality. A great weakness of the psychoanalytic argument is that it lessens the story's artistic effect. There are logical difficulties as well.

What Siegel does is to tackle the content of the evil that is felt, as James intended it to be felt, by the reader. There *is* a feeling of evil. Even if you can't say what it is, there is something in your mind. What is it? The critical problem is to describe the evil in a way that accounts for the story's effect without weakening it.

The basis of Siegel's explanation is in the ethics of Aesthetic Realism, specifically in the concept of contempt as an unconscious force. It is well known that a person gets some satisfaction out of being able to despise another. But the extent of the desire for this satisfaction and what it leads to, are not known, and usually not believed when seen. The beginning of contempt is described in the *Four Statements:* "a disposition in every person to think he will be for himself by making less of the outside world." Now, that doesn't sound so awfully bad, does it? But it can be shown that if it were not for this disposition, there would be no lying, no stealing, no cruelty, no murder.

Siegel discusses evil both from the point of view of where it begins in time and where it begins in terms of form. He shows that evil doesn't begin when you "do" something, it begins with thought; and further, that it was Henry James's fascination with a kind of thought as having in it the beginning of good and evil which it was his lifelong work and great distinction to embody in works of fiction.

The significance of Siegel's criticism is that an exploration and discovery in the field of ethics and religion is coherent with an exploration and discovery in terms of literary style: the value of Henry James as an artist. What makes this coherence possible is the Aesthetic Realism way of seeing opposites. One of the things that will be found, particularly as the story approaches its *dénouement,* is that opposites, sensitively observed, explain the characters—especially that of the governess—and make what happens understandable.

So, while Siegel's interpretation is in keeping with the way the story has been taken by the customary reader (that is, the governess is believed), his presentation of its meaning, its artistic excellence, and the reason it has affected people so powerfully — on these points, his criticism is different from any that has been.

Eli Siegel is, in my opinion, the first critic of our age. He has found and stated the thing common to all instances of art: "the oneness of the permanent opposites in reality as seen by an individual." As a teacher, he has demonstrated the superb flexibility and accuracy of this principle in literally thousands of specific poems, plays, novels, short stories, essays. Never have I known anyone so able to make books live, to make their import stir *within* a person. He lessens the distance between print and life. And through what means? First of all, respect for the word. He looks at what each word says *exactly,* and then (which by no means always follows) is able to see the meaning, including nuances and aromas, of one word going with another. This happens with *The Turn of the Screw.* The person who hears or reads Siegel's criticism has a new experience in seeing what a book—a quiet book—can do.

The lectures were given, as was said, in 1953. For many who heard them, they were decisive in revealing James as a writer to be loved. They stimulated a vast reading in his works, and they were remembered. In 1966, excerpts from the James talks were given as dramatic readings at the Terrain Gallery by a cast of three. In 1967, the series was repeated.

This work is based on the Terrain Gallery readings, given in four parts. I made selections from transcripts of the recorded talks—24 in all. They were "talks"— that is, prepared carefully but given extemporaneously. Siegel does not write out what he is going to say, or read from little cards, or memorize fine strokes ahead of time. He *talks*. The editing was done with a desire to preserve this quality. Because much is omitted, it has been necessary occasionally in the body of the work to insert an editorial note for clarity or continuity.

A word about Mrs. Grose, the housekeeper. As Hart says, she never sees the ghosts herself, but—as he does not say—she identifies them as Quint and Jessel from the governess' description. The flavor of Mrs. Grose's character and her relation to the governess is not given at all by his condescending description of her as "this kindly, simple woman" whom the governess has some-how "won" to "her cause." Siegel pointed out that Mrs. Grose is to the governess a little as Horatio is to Hamlet and Sancho Panza is to Don Quixote: the solid, good, ordinary person, not as sensitive as the other, but who follows along.

Siegel gave a very full discussion of James's other works and their interrelations, and through this came, little by little, an understanding of James's "way," so uniquely present in *The Turn of the Screw*. Some of the most salient passages of the preliminary "hovering" have been selected and comprise the first section of the present work. These are principally the discussions of *What Maisie Knew* and two of James's lesser known stories, "Maud-Evelyn" and "The Pupil."

I wish to thank Anne Fielding, Sheldon Kranz, and Nancy Starrels, the original cast of *James and the Children* at the Terrain Gallery, and Dorothy Koppelman, the gallery's director, for suggestions and encouragement in the preparation of this manuscript.

MARTHA BAIRD

1

Careful Hovering

As YOU may have gathered by now, the viewpoint of
Aesthetic Realism as to *The Turn of the Screw* is that
the children weren't so good; and further, that though
they may have been badly affected by those two
shadowy figures, the governess and the handyman who
are now dead, they also had evil in them. It is an evil
that can be studied in the works of James's father and
also in the works of the teacher of James's father,
Swedenborg. The children, Miles and Flora, represent
evil; and what is necessary to see is that children can,
and that they also can represent innocence. This is important because it tells us what we are.

Since in *The Turn of the Screw*, the ethics of man as
presented through the children is so important, it is
well to bring as many supporting things for the Aesthetic Realism viewpoint as can be.

There is a poem by Blake in which a child is seen
as sulky and evil and "individual" in a bad way. This
poem is in two versions; there is one in the Rossetti
Manuscripts with quite a few stanzas where the child
complains a great deal of what it got into and how it's
going to meet it; and then there is a version in Blake's

Songs of Experience. In the *Songs of Experience*, the poem is called "Infant Sorrow." (Blake, by the way, was very much affected by Swedenborg, though he wrote notes against him.) This is Blake's "Infant Sorrow":

> My mother groan'd, my father wept,
> Into the dangerous world I leapt;
> Helpless, naked, piping loud,
> Like a fiend hid in a cloud.
>
> Struggling in my father's hands,
> Striving against my swaddling-bands,
> Bound and weary, I thought best
> To sulk upon my mother's breast.

Well, that child doesn't look too cherubic. He's a terror. And there are more details in the longer version.

There are quite a few poems on the innocence of the child, the most famous of which is Wordsworth's "Intimations of Immortality." Another is by Henry Vaughan of the 17th century. This is from Vaughan's "The Retreate"; it shows the divinity of the child:

> Happy those early dayes! when I
> Shin'd in my Angell-infancy.
> Before I understood this place
> Appointed for my second race,
> Or taught my soul to fancy ought
> But a white, Celestiall thought.

You wouldn't think Vaughan and Blake were writing on the same subject, but they really are. Both poems represent something in the child: the child is angelic and intolerable. Aesthetic Realism believes that the way children are innocent and also intolerable is something that has to be looked at.

I shall deal first with *What Maisie Knew*, because there a child represents something good, though she also fumbles. In *What Maisie Knew*, one can see James's attitude to parents. It is an implication of mine that the children in *The Turn of the Screw* did not care too much for their parents, though the parents have died and aren't around. Miles and Flora, being aristocratic children, get a certain satisfaction from patronizing two servants, as rich boys and girls—and even not so rich boys and girls—have done in the past. These two children have a contempt for adults which Maisie also has, but she doesn't use it to hope to have contempt for everything. There is the difference.

The having of contempt, as I have said pretty often, is not a bad thing. After all, things will act contemptibly, so what can you do? But to *hope* that they act contemptibly and to use persons' weakness to exalt oneself, is bad. Maisie has contempt for a lot of things, but she doesn't try to exploit it, and she doesn't fool herself. She is a very knowing child; she is just as keen as Flora and Miles, maybe even a little keener. But she doesn't use the weakness of adults to get herself a bad glory, as Miles and Flora do.

A child is presented terrifyingly and sweetly in *What Maisie Knew*. This book was published a year before *The Turn of the Screw*, that is, 1897; and it hasn't been taken, as far as I know, seriously enough. It is one of the most terrific evaluations of the family—father and mother—that has ever appeared. And it is interesting that James should write this not as a young man—young men, for instance, have written novels about fathers or uncles interfering with their artistic endeavors and such things. But that James should write this way fairly on in life is mighty interesting. The question is, what did Maisie know? James doesn't say. The book ends as follows:

> Mrs. Wix also was silent a while. "He went to *her*," she finally observed.
> "Oh I know!" the child replied.
> Mrs. Wix gave a sidelong look. She still had room for wonder at what Maisie knew.

One of the things that Maisie knew was the weakness of adults; the other thing that Maisie knew was what James knew, what an artist knows in varying degrees: how things could be beautiful. In other words, Maisie was a critic, but she didn't use her criticism or contempt to spoil her notion of beauty, as the other children did.

First of all, *What Maisie Knew* deals with a man and wife, the Faranges, who disagree. They are Maisie's parents. James as usual doesn't say wholly what they disagreed about. That's not his way; he wants to be devastating through vagueness. But you feel other people concerned. Ida and Beale Farange do openly hate each other. So they have a divorce, and Maisie is supposed to be six months with the mother and six months with the father. Of course that already is a little difficult. She is supposed to be tossed from one person to another, both of whom hate each other.

Mother and father can use a child as a means of asserting their own vanities. This goes on a great deal in family life. James knows that it does. Why did the Faranges want a child? James says:

They had wanted her not for any good they could do her, but for the harm they could, with her unconscious aid, do each other.

That is very strong. The beginning of *What Maisie Knew* is not James using his finger tips: he's going around angry.

So these two people have used the child against each other. It happens very frequently. The feelings they have are quite terrible. James says:

> The mother had wished to prevent the father from, as she said, "so much as looking" at the child; the father's plea was that the mother's lightest touch was "simply contamination."

Most people are not divorced, but this kind of feeling, which James presents straight and terribly, is had. Mothers have said, "Don't bother the child, take your hands off him," with all kinds of implications.

And so Maisie goes first to her father. And the mother writes letters:

> Her first term was with her father, who spared her only in not letting her have the wild letters addressed to her by her mother: he confined himself to holding them up at her and shaking them, while he showed his teeth, and then amusing her by the way he chucked them, across the room, bang into the fire. Even at that moment, however, she had a scared anticipation of fatigue, a guilty sense of not rising to the occasion, feeling the charm of the violence with which the stiff unopened envelopes, whose big monograms —Ida bristled with monograms—she would have liked to see, were made to whizz, like dangerous missiles, through the air.

All this is in front of the child; and she did have a very good chance of becoming a sour and concealed fright.

She doesn't say what is on her mind, but it's not for the purpose of deceiving. She is still looking for something that is beautiful.

The servants here are important, because what often happens is that if mother and father are disagreeing, the servants know it. They conceal their disrespect, of course, as employees very often do with the boss.

Maisie has two governesses in time. (There are two also in *The Turn of the Screw*.) We have a feeling of the relation of servants. You may remember that the governess in *The Turn of the Screw* is immediately seen as somewhat loftier than Mrs. Grose, the housekeeper, or the other servants. Here there is a comparison between the governess, Miss Overmore, and Moddle, the nurse:

> Miss Overmore, however hungry, never disappeared: this marked her somehow as of higher rank, and the character was confirmed by a prettiness that Maisie supposed to be extraordinary.

Maisie's mother, Mrs. Farange, is richly detestable. She uses all the mother's business. Every now and then she will hug Maisie to herself effusively: "How can I live without you? Can you still care for your dear, dear mother though that awful Mr. Farange keeps you away from me?" And in the meantime, she is going on with her pursuits. All this is vague, but Mrs. Farange, it seems, is pretty effective with gentlemen. This is punctuated with her huggings and claspings and sobbings towards Maisie. Occasionally Mrs. Farange shows herself very sarcastic. Maisie has just said, "Oh I thought she was."

> "It doesn't in the least matter, you know, what you think," Mrs. Farange loudly replied; "and you had better

indeed for the future, miss, learn to keep your thoughts to yourself." This was exactly what Maisie had already learned, and the accomplishment was just the source of her mother's irritation.

Two frequent remarks of mothers are: "Don't prattle so much, dear," and, "You never tell your mother anything." But Maisie is judging her elders in general, not just her parents:

> It was of a horrid little critical system, a tendency, in her silence, to judge her elders, that this lady suspected her, liking as she did, for her own part, a child to be simple and confiding.

Her mother saw that Maisie had thoughts that were critical. She didn't want to know what they were, but she was angry that Maisie dared to have them. Adults don't like children to have thoughts about them: it is very annoying. But if people are going to have children, they might as well get used to it.

Maisie gets very fond of Miss Overmore. She wants to like somebody very much.

> She had conceived her first passion, and the object of it was her governess. It hadn't been put to her, and she couldn't, or at any rate she didn't, put it to herself, that she liked Miss Overmore better than she liked papa; but it would have sustained her under such an imputation to feel herself able to reply that papa too liked Miss Overmore exactly as much. He had particularly told her so. Besides she could easily see it.

The fact that Maisie likes Miss Overmore better than she likes papa is quite clearly related to what goes on in *The Turn of the Screw.* The children didn't have parents about, so they couldn't like them, but the fact re-

mains that they settled on Miss Jessel, the governess,
and Quint, the man useful around the house. James says
Maisie felt she liked Miss Overmore, the governess,
better than her father. That is already important.

And then there is a distinction between concealment
and deception. When you conceal a thing because you
don't want a person to meddle with the truth or to alter
it or deface it or defile it or misjudge it or disrespect it,
you are not deceiving, because your purpose is to maintain the truth. But if you say something for the purpose
of someone else not ever seeing the truth, that is deception. James makes the distinction in a way:

> For Maisie moreover concealment had never necessarily
> seemed deception; she had grown up among things as to
> which her foremost knowledge was that she was never to
> ask about them.

Sometimes Maisie tries to say what's on her mind,
but she very often doesn't fare so well. There is a description of her difficulty:

> The child's discipline had been bewildering — it had
> ranged freely between the prescription that she was to
> answer when spoken to and the experience of lively
> penalties on obeying that prescription.

We have a relation of the quadrilateral and the six:
the governess, Miss Overmore, marries Maisie's father
and becomes Mrs. Beale Farange; and then Sir Claude
marries Ida Farange, Maisie's mother; then after a while
the governess is interested in Sir Claude and Sir Claude
in the governess. And there is another governess, Mrs.
Wix, who represents an intense but not so flexible attitude to morality. I think James is satirizing his father a

little bit here. But that is not the chief thing about Mrs. Wix.

So Maisie in a way gets two new parents, Miss Overmore and Sir Claude; and then they in turn become interested in each other. Towards the end of the book, she shows her criticism of that interest: she wants her stepfather, Sir Claude, to give up Miss Overmore. There is some geometrical symbolism; and many things of depth and vagueness and subtlety are here.

Sir Claude is very interested in Maisie. He has questions about himself, and he feels that he can find an answer in Maisie. She represents wisdom and art. He says:

> "If you'll help me, you know, I'll help *you*," he concluded in the pleasant fraternising, equalising, not a bit patronising way which made the child ready to go through anything for him and the beauty of which, as she dimly felt, was that it was so much less a deceitful descent to her years than a real indifference to them.

That is very refreshing. She is talked to as a person, not patronizingly. Many people think children want to be patronized. Yes, they will be, they want to be, because they can use it, they can get a lot of importance from it; but there is something that every child not entirely straight from hell wants more. What happens when somebody patronizes a child is that the child in turn does some patronizing of the adults.

There is some interesting conversation between Maisie and Sir Claude:

> "How can I help it?" Maisie enquired in surprise. "Mamma doesn't care for me," she said very simply. "Not really." Child as she was, her little long history was in the

words; and it was as impossible to contradict her as if she had been venerable.

Many children could say that. But then, it is all confused by the fact that the mother has such a deep meaning; and the fact, too, that the mother doesn't care for one enough is a big wound: it is a wound that can't be explained.

There is a description of more of the contradictoriness of Mrs. Farange:

> But she was a person addicted to extremes—sometimes barely speaking to her child and sometimes pressing this tender shoot to a bosom cut, as Mrs. Wix had also observed, remarkably low.

That is James quite satirical, and neatly so.

At one time four adults come together, and as usual James goes after Ida:

> This was the very moral of a scene that flashed into vividness one day when the four happened to meet without company in the drawing-room and Maisie found herself clutched to her mother's breast and passionately sobbed and shrieked over, made the subject of a demonstration evidently sequent to some sharp passage just enacted.

In other words, when Ida Farange didn't do so well with other people, suddenly she became *very* affectionate to Maisie. She found time then to show how good a mother she was. But Maisie doesn't come through; she begins getting a little suspicious of this sobbing and clasping. And then Ida Farange gets angry:

> "I'm very good to break my heart about it when you've no more feeling for me than a clammy little fish!" She

suddenly thrust the child away and, as a disgusted admission of failure, sent her flying across the room into the arms of Mrs. Wix, whom at this moment and even in the whirl of her transit Maisie saw, very red, exchange a quick queer look with Sir Claude.

This is fierce. I have never seen anything so fierce about the insincerity of parentage. I think people have been afraid to tackle this, afraid to see the meaning of this book: it definitely explains certain aspects of *The Turn of the Screw.*

All this shows that James had anger. The way he deals with Mrs. Farange is angry. This is important, because James could appear angelic, very quiet, beatific; and if we forget that he also was in a rage—and sometimes a lucid rage—we cannot understand the full nature of *The Turn of the Screw:* how he is pleased with the children and also angry with them.

Maisie represents art in a child: the desire to know good and evil in their true relation. Maisie is not given to the idea of power through aloofness. Miles and Flora, I think, are. Maisie wants to find out things, and to find out, she uses "little silences" and "intelligent little looks," and so she gets "delightful little glimpses." James says:

> She learned on the other hand soon to recognize how at last, sometimes, patient little silences and intelligent little looks could be rewarded by delightful little glimpses.

Maisie wants people to be good; and when there is a sign, she is very affected and has a tendency to tears— but they are good tears:

> The tears came into her eyes again as they had done when in the Park that day the Captain told her so "splendidly" that her mother was good.

She wants to see people as good, and you can ask yourself whether the children in *The Turn of the Screw* do.
I do not think so; and a good person wants people to be
good. That is one of the big indications.

Maisie as artist is aware of the thoughts of people
about other people. There is a strange passage which is
akin to other passages in James, about people's vision of
other people's vision of people.

> The immensity didn't include *them;* but if he had an
> idea at the back of his head she had also one in a recess
> as deep, and for a time, while they sat together, there was
> an extraordinary mute passage between her vision of this
> vision of his, his vision of her vision, and her vision of his
> vision of her vision.

Why shouldn't there be? That's what feelings do: you
can think of another person thinking of another person
thinking of you. That's what mind can do, and James is
aware of it. You can have a vision of another person's
vision of another person's vision of you. James has reminded us of this.

The attempt in *What Maisie Knew* is to show the
grandeur, the necessity of knowing. Maisie does feel
herself to be a good influence on adults. There is an
intimation that Maisie can bring more form to adults'
lives, and this is one passage showing it:

> Mrs. Wix was in truth more than ever qualified to meet
> embarrassment; I am not sure that Maisie had not even a
> dim discernment of the queer law of her own life that
> made her educate to that sort of proficiency those elders
> with whom she was concerned. She promoted, as it were,
> their development; nothing could have been more marked
> for instance than her success in promoting Mrs. Beale's.

This is not the time to go into any long statement on
how children can teach their parents, but they can.

James saw a person who did not want to know as a villain—that's what it came to: as a person who could be looked upon as representing evil. James saw knowing as being art because, as Aesthetic Realism would put it, knowledge is complete when feeling is of it: when logic and emotion are one. And when that knowledge occurs, it is akin to art.

As I see it, when James had presented a child in the art way, the beautiful way, Maisie, he was ready to tackle the other thing in children. And so there is a reason *The Turn of the Screw* should have been thought about after *What Maisie Knew*. The two are related. Maisie is the aesthetic ideal, in all her interesting and profound youthfulness. If the book is read that way and thought of in relation to *The Turn of the Screw*, I think the upshot of *The Turn of the Screw* will be seen better.

Mrs. Wix talks to Maisie about Mrs. Beale and Sir Claude. It has been felt that James questioned love even more severely than Freud did. Some of the fiercest statements about love are made by James, in this book and elsewhere. Mrs. Wix talks about what Mrs. Beale wants of Sir Claude; she says:

> "Do you want to know really and truly why? So that she may be his wretchedness and his punishment."
> "His punishment?"—this was more than as yet Maisie could quite accept. "For what?"
> "For everything. That's what will happen: he'll be tied to her for ever. She won't mind in the least his hating her, and she won't hate him back."

This notion of love that Mrs. Wix expresses has to do with James's own. It is not consummate, it is not complete, but it has to be known before the complete is seen.

A good deal in James is about people loving dead people—or people that don't even exist. That is akin to something in Poe I've talked about pretty often. The most beautiful person for Poe was a dead woman showing signs of life, or a live woman ready to die. Apparently he couldn't love anybody unless that person were close to death in some fashion. This is strong in James too, but it doesn't take the form that it takes in Poe. In James it's a deeper thing; in fact, the moral of James's works could be put this way: Love only live people, but to do this, you have to be alive yourself. This can be seen in James's ghostly stories and in his stories generally.

The idea, which is tremendous in its terror, of people wanting to love others only when they are nothing, only when they are annihilated, only when they are not present—this has to do with *The Turn of the Screw;* and there are intimations of it in *What Maisie Knew.* Sir Claude talks in a way that makes him seem not the man of pleasure that some persons take him to be. He says:

> "I've not killed anything," he said; "on the contrary I think I've produced life. I don't know what to call it—I haven't even known how decently to deal with it, to approach it; but, whatever it is, it's the most beautiful thing I've ever met—it's exquisite, it's sacred."

There is a feeling in James that corresponds to the oldtime notion of vampire: that there exists something like a vampire in people. The vampire did exist, particularly in the Balkan states; and in Greece there were vampires. They came to suck your blood. The vampire was dealt with by Kipling, and it has been elsewhere. Strindberg's women are mostly vampires, though he doesn't call them that. James was very much taken with the idea, and perhaps his least successful work, *The Sacred Fount,* deals with how, because someone was married to someone, he gets much older, more pallid, and frail. The idea is that you take over the life principle of somebody else, and in the meantime the other person gets languid.

This idea was in James as it was in Nietzsche and Schopenhauer and Strindberg: that people, under the guise of love, really take the life from someone. James presents it in *The Sacred Fount* and elsewhere in a subtle and roundabout fashion. People have been appalled by *The Sacred Fount:* what *was* happening in that book?

So Sir Claude's saying, "I've not killed anything," is very meaningful.

Then there is a quarrel between Mrs. Wix and Mrs. Beale. Mrs. Beale wants Maisie for her purposes; Mrs. Wix also wants Maisie. Mrs. Beale is more flashy.

One of the things that makes me think that Flora is not an ideal Reynolds child, that she is not Miss Innocence misled by governesses, is the fact that she gets so ill-mannered. It is like the way Mrs. Beale gets ill-mannered.

Well, this is about the quarrel. It is about the choice: with whom is Maisie to go, with Mrs. Beale and Sir Claude or with Mrs. Wix? Maisie says that unless Mrs. Beale and Sir Claude separate, she won't go with Sir Claude. With Sir Claude alone, or not at all.

Somehow, now that it was there, the great moment was not so bad. What helped the child was that she knew what she wanted. All her learning and learning had made her at last learn that; so that if she waited an instant to reply it was only from the desire to be nice. Bewilderment had simply gone or at any rate was going fast. Finally she answered. "Will you give *him* up? Will you?"

"Ah leave her alone—leave her, leave her!" Sir Claude in sudden supplication murmured to Mrs. Beale.

Mrs. Wix at the same instant found another apostrophe. "Isn't it enough for you, madam, to have brought her to discussing your relations?"

Mrs. Beale left Sir Claude unheeded, but Mrs. Wix could make her flame.

Mrs. Beale has been rather sweet so far, just as Flora is sweet up until she turns on the governess when the governess bothers her too much; but now that Mrs. Wix has really annoyed her, she shows that she is not just a lady. This is Mrs. Beale to Mrs. Wix:

"My relations? What do you know, you hideous creature, about my relations, and what business on earth have you to speak of them? Leave the room this instant, you horrible old woman!"

"I think you had better go—you must really catch your boat," Sir Claude said distressfully to Mrs. Wix. He was out of it now, or wanted to be; he knew the worst and had accepted it: what now concerned him was to prevent, to dissipate vulgarities. "Won't you go—won't you just get off quickly?"

"With the child as quickly as you like. Not without her." Mrs. Wix was adamant.

"Then why did you lie to me, you fiend?" Mrs. Beale almost yelled. "Why did you tell me an hour ago that you had given her up?"

"Because I despaired of her—because I thought she had left me." Mrs. Wix turned to Maisie. "You were *with* them—in their connexion. But now your eyes are open, and I take you!"

"No, you don't!" and Mrs. Beale made, with a great fierce jump, a wild snatch at her stepdaughter. She caught her by the arm and, completing an instinctive movement, whirled her round in a further leap to the door, which

had been closed by Sir Claude the instant their voices had
risen. She fell back against it and, even while denouncing
and waving off Mrs. Wix, kept it closed in an incoherence
of passion. "You don't take her, but you bundle yourself:
she stays with her own people and she's rid of you! I
never heard anything so monstrous!" Sir Claude had
rescued Maisie and kept hold of her; he held her in front
of him, resting his hands very lightly on her shoulders and
facing the four adversaries. Mrs. Beale's flush had
dropped; she had turned pale with a splendid wrath. She
kept protesting and dismissing Mrs. Wix; she glued her
back to the door to prevent Maisie's flight; she drove out
Mrs. Wix by the window or the chimney. "You're a nice
one—'discussing relations'—with your talk of our 'connexion' and your insults! What in the world's our connexion but the love of the child who's our duty and our
life and who holds us together as closely as she originally
brought us?"

Then Maisie still wants her point: she'll go with Sir
Claude but she'll go only with him, not with him and
Mrs. Beale. Mrs. Beale now includes Maisie in her anger.
Before then she had been very careful, but now that
she is wrathful, she includes Maisie too:

> "*Will* you give him up?" Maisie persisted to Mrs. Beale.
> "To *you,* you abominable little horror?" the lady in-
> dignantly enquired, "and to this raving old demon who
> has filled your dreadful little mind with her wickedness?
> Have you been a hideous little hypocrite all these years
> that I've slaved to make you love me and deludedly be-
> lieved you did?"
> "I love Sir Claude—I love *him,*" Maisie replied with an
> awkward sense that she appeared to offer it as something
> that would do as well. Sir Claude had continued to pat
> her, and it was really an answer to his pats.

She's not so sure of Sir Claude either, now; but Maisie
sticks to her point:

Maisie looked at her with new eyes, but answered as she had answered before. "Will you give him up?"

Mrs. Beale's rejoinder hung fire, but when it came it was noble. "You shouldn't talk to me of such things!" She was shocked, she was scandalized to tears.

Then towards the very end:

Sir Claude had reached the other door and opened it. Mrs. Wix was already out. On the threshold Maisie paused; she put out her hand to her stepfather. He took it and held it a moment, and their eyes met as the eyes of those who have done for each other what they can. "Good-bye," he repeated.

And she goes with Mrs. Wix. Not, I think, deeply or entirely, but because in Mrs. Wix there hasn't been any arrant falsity. The very last sentences of the book I read before; they are:

Mrs. Wix also was silent a while. "He went to *her*." she finally observed.

"Oh I know!" the child replied.

Mrs. Wix gave a sidelong look. She still had room for wonder at what Maisie knew.

What Maisie knew is about art and evil. She has seen a very great deal of it, and she wants her knowledge to help people.

Before I get to the text of *The Turn of the Screw*, I want to comment on the story of "Maud-Evelyn," which is one of the most misunderstood stories. I see it as one of the most terrible. It seems very dullish, but it is about how people don't want to love each other until they make each other into nothing: annihilate them and then love them. The story seems very tepid, very Westbourne Terrace, but it is terrible. It is the terrible changed into the tepid; the fierce changed into the lukewarm.

The dull person in "Maud-Evelyn" is Marmaduke; he is called a "crown prince," as we'll see. He, of all people, a crown prince! He is like dishwater in the sun for three days. Marmaduke is a person who wants to vanish; he wants to be completely flat, so that no one can see him. But he also wants to be able to make other people flat. It is a strange story; it is even comic; but James does have terror and the comic join.

Marmaduke has been taken over by two people, the Dedricks, who had a daughter that died, and they are giving their whole life to her memory. She is Maud-Evelyn. Lady Emma, who is telling the story, asks Marmaduke:

> "But are you," I asked, "as fond of them—"
> "As they are of *me?*" He took me up promptly, and his eyes were quite unclouded. "I'm quite sure I shall become so."

But you feel that Marmaduke really doesn't want to.

There is talk of making use of people. Lady Emma sees Marmaduke as either getting softening of the brain or as very cunning and wanting a fortune by taking up these people with their dead daughter, whom they venerate and go to mediums about. Marmaduke joins the Dedricks and their dead daughter, and it seems that in a way he gets to marry the dead daughter. The girl he knows, Lavinia, doesn't mind, because she gets something out of it. It is very strange, put this way: how people want to make nothing of each other, and "as long as you're nothing, I'll love you." You either have to be flat or nothing.

The terrible import of this story I'm afraid, has not been seen. Marmaduke is just seen as a nebbish. But the process of taking the life out of people and wanting live things not to be alive, is there.

You can see that the person telling the story, Lady Emma, doesn't like Marmaduke. She wants Lavinia to see him right, but Lavinia is no bargain either.

> She demurred a little. "But why?"
> "So that at least he shan't make use of you," I said with energy.

And the Dedricks are making use of Marmaduke too. There is an interesting description of Lavinia. It's a little complicated, and I don't think it gets over too well; but while Marmaduke has almost attained to nothing, she has attained to flatness. Lady Emma says:

> There were mixed in her then, in a puzzling way, two qualities that mostly exclude each other — an extreme timidity and, as the smallest fault that could qualify a harmless creature for a world of wickedness, a self-complacency hard in tiny, unexpected spots, for which I used sometimes to take her up, but which, I subsequently saw, would have done something for the flatness of her life had they not evaporated with everything else.

It seems that Lavinia is trying to be important by having herself completely out of sight. In the process, she takes the guts out of the world, and so does Marmaduke.

The Dedricks are queer: they give their lives to a dead child. It sounds noble, but James thinks that it isn't, and the character telling the story doesn't think it is either. The dead child, Maud-Evelyn, is described as "incontestably beautiful." You must remember that

Flora was incontestably beautiful too. This is about the Dedricks:

> Their feeling had drawn to itself their whole conscious-
> ness; it had become mildly maniacal. The idea was fixed,
> and it kept others out. The world, for the most part,
> allows no leisure for such a ritual, but the world had
> consistently neglected this plain, shy couple, who were
> sensitive to the wrong things and whose sincerity and
> fidelity, as well as their tameness and twaddle, were of a
> rigid, antique pattern.

James doesn't say how much he detests these people, but you can see he doesn't like them. Lady Emma says, "I don't want to meet these people." When Marmaduke asks her, "Meet my friends," she doesn't want to. James shows how he feels in his quiet manner, but it's definite.

Some of Marmaduke's attitude—how he is for death —is to be seen in these sentences:

> His reply had been abundant and imperturbable—had in-
> cluded some glance at the way death brings into relief
> even the faintest things that have preceded it; on which
> I felt myself suddenly as restless as if I had grown afraid
> of him. I got up to ring for tea; he went on talking —
> talking about Maud-Evelyn and what she had been for
> him; and when the servant had come up I prolonged,
> nervously, on purpose, the order I had wished to give.

Then Marmaduke is called a crown prince. After the Dedricks marry Marmaduke to the dead girl, they die themselves—their work is over; and they leave their property to Marmaduke.

> He "talked" like a crown prince. "They were ready, to
> the last touch—there was nothing more to be done. And

they're just as they were—not an object moved, not an arrangement altered, not a person but ourselves coming in: they're only exquisitely kept. All our presents are there—I should have liked you to see them."

The story could have as a subtitle: The Epic of Selfish Drips. The people are that way. It's all presented in stucco, with dullness; and I don't think James knew what he was dealing with.

James took children very seriously; and as a means of understanding the governess' position, I believe it is well to mention another story, "The Pupil," and comment on it.

In "The Pupil," there is a person named Pemberton, just out of Oxford. He has done well at Oxford, and he meets this family, the Moreens, who are quite shady, very much interested in their own advancement — particularly the father and mother. Then there are two daughters and another son, and there is this boy, Morgan. He is decidedly keen—a "genius," so it is said. The mother talks about Pemberton's being a tutor for this boy, and she is vague, especially about the money part of it. But he becomes the tutor.

Morgan, who is a much better boy than Miles (he is older too), does not care for his family—in fact, he says his family is no good—and he wants to go away with Pemberton. He is very friendly with Pemberton. But when he has a chance to go away with Pemberton, he finds it too hard, and he also dies of a heart attack, as Miles does.

One thing in bad ethics is trying to maintain a bad equilibrium between two things. People do that. It is a phase of compromise. One way of compromise is blankness, flatness, abstinence: you don't do anything, you do nothing, nothing at all. And the other way is to juggle two things conveniently.

Now, the boy in this story is much more likable than Miles. Morgan does come out with his abhorrence of his father and mother and the rest of his family, and it is very taking; but we feel there is an uncertainty. There is also an uncertainty about Pemberton. Pemberton is a little like Winterbourne in *Daisy Miller:* he makes certain things clear to Daisy, but he isn't clear enough. "The Pupil" is a story of uncertainty. One feels that the boy, though he despised his family, also could not get away from them.

It is well, then, in this study of *The Turn of the Screw,* to look a bit at this story. There is a relation among Miles and Flora, who definitely want to use people; Morgan, who wants to become free and hopes that he can; and then Maisie, who has made up her mind in a good way. There is a relation among the three.

There are no ghosts in "The Pupil"; there are the parents, and Pemberton, and the other children. Pemberton says towards the end of the story, after Morgan's death:

> "He couldn't stand it with his weak organ," said Pemberton—"the shock, the whole scene, the violent emotion."
>
> "But I thought he *wanted* to go to you!" wailed Mrs. Moreen.
>
> "I *told* you he didn't, my dear," her husband made answer. Mr. Moreen was trembling all over and was in his way as deeply affected as his wife. But after the very first he took his bereavement as a man of the world.

There is a kinship of this ending to the ending of *Daisy Miller:* Winterbourne takes Daisy's death pretty deeply, but he also goes on.

If we look at this story, we see that, with less passion than in *The Turn of the Screw* and, I think, with less aesthetic effect, the things that children go through are dealt with. The fact that Morgan found some satisfaction in despising his parents is not stated. Morgan is likable; he has a big desire to be honest, but everything doesn't permit him. He doesn't make it.

Let us take this bit, Morgan and Pemberton:

> They were silent a minute; after which the boy asked: "Do you like my father and mother very much?"
> "Dear me, yes. Charming people."
> Morgan received this with another silence; then unexpectedly, familiarly, but at the same time affectionately, he remarked: "You're a jolly old humbug!"

Pemberton feels that if he's teaching the boy, he shouldn't say anything against the parents; he has some sensitivities.

> What had added to the clumsiness then was that he thought it his duty to declare to Morgan that he might abuse him, Pemberton, as much as he liked, but must never abuse his parents. To this Morgan had the easy retort that he hadn't dreamed of abusing them; which appeared to be true: it put Pemberton in the wrong.

That is, Morgan says things against his parents, but he thinks it is not abusing them at all. Pemberton is trying to accept a very unusual situation, where a boy definitely is aware that something is wrong with his parents and *wants* to talk about it like nobody's business. It is partly received by Pemberton, but Pemberton doesn't see the whole meaning of it. It would be interesting to compare Pemberton with the governess.

There are some other passages worth noting. What happens is this: the parents, knowing that Pemberton

is very fond of their son, feel that since he is fond of
their son, why should they pay him? He gets enough
from having such good company, their wonderful boy.
They want to put aside the boy, but they also want to
hold on to him. It is very interesting to see how much
they are fond of him, yet how they want to give him
over to somebody else. After the boy does go to Pemberton, his clothes become not as good as they used to
be—that is, Mrs. Moreen saves money on him:

> He could trace perfectly the degrees by which, in pro-
> portion as her little son confined himself to his tutor for
> society, Mrs. Moreen shrewdly forbore to renew his gar-
> ments.

We see the calculation on the part of the parents,
and it is much more in the open than some of the
things in *What Maisie Knew*. The Moreens care for
their son but they also want to use their son. Parents
have used children for their glory. We have this sentence:

> Wasn't he paid enough without perpetual money—wasn't
> he paid by the comfortable luxurious home he enjoyed
> with them all, without a care, an anxiety, a solitary want?

This negative way of seeing people—"Don't you get
something out of it already?"—is said by James to be
bad ethics. It's a way of saying that because an actor
liked doing his work, enjoyed it, therefore the being
praised and the enjoyment was enough of a payment.
Payment has a great deal to do with ethics, and "The
Pupil" is a story about the nature of payment, partly.

There is an interesting anecdote about how the parents used the boy in his relation with a nurse, and also
about how they wanted to use the nurse. Morgan is very

plain about his parents. What we feel here, however, is that while the boy wants to be honest about his parents, the tendency to despise them is something he might luxuriate in. James isn't definite enough about this.

Pemberton now has permission to talk to the boy about his parents:

A couple of days after this, during which he had failed to profit by so free a permission, he had been for a quarter of an hour walking with his charge in silence when the boy became sociable again with the remark: "I'll tell you how I know it; I know it through Zénobie."

"Zénobie? Who in the world is *she?*"

"A nurse I used to have—ever so many years ago. A charming woman. I liked her awfully, and she liked me."

"There's no accounting for tastes. What is it you know through her?"

"Why what their idea is. She went away because they didn't fork out. She did like me awfully, and she stayed two years. She told me all about it—that at last she could never get her wages. As soon as they saw how much she liked me they stopped giving her anything. They thought she'd stay for nothing—just *because,* don't you know?" And Morgan had a queer little conscious lucid look. "She did stay ever so long—as long as she could. She was only a poor girl. She used to send money to her mother. At last she couldn't afford it any longer, and went away in a fearful rage one night—I mean of course in a rage against *them.* She cried over me tremendously, she hugged me nearly to death. She told me all about it," the boy repeated. "She told me it was their idea. So I guessed, ever so long ago, that they have had the same idea with you."

"Zénobie was very sharp," said Pemberton. "And she made you so."

"Oh that wasn't Zénobie; that was nature. And experience!" Morgan laughed.

"Well, Zénobie was a part of your experience."

"Certainly I was a part of hers, poor dear!" the boy wisely sighed. "And I'm part of yours."

This has a relation of passive and active, for it seems he affected her too. We get these little touches. Morgan is nice, but he is aware that he is affecting people too. He can be satirical. He knows there's something wrong: he feels he's wrong, Pemberton is wrong, and his parents are wrong.

> Morgan went on in silence, for a moment. Then he said: "My dear chap, you're a hero!"
> "Well, you're another!" Pemberton retorted.
> "No I'm not, but I ain't a baby. I won't stand it any longer. You must get some occupation that pays. I'm ashamed, I'm ashamed!" quavered the boy with a ring of passion, like some high silver note from a small cathedral chorister, that deeply touched his friend.

I'm reading this in order to show that James was ready to give notions of good and evil to children, and also felt that they could express them. He is one of the few writers who can do that. We can see three kinds of children, all having to do with the good and evil problem: Maisie, the best; Morgan, undecided; and then Flora and Miles. When we study the ways of speech of the three groups or three kinds of children, I think we can get closer to being sure what James's *Turn of the Screw* is about.

Morgan is talking about his parents:

> "I'm not proud of *them*. But you know that," Morgan returned.
> "Except for the little matter we speak of they're charming people," said Pemberton, not taking up the point made for his intelligence, but wondering greatly at the boy's own, and especially at this fresh reminder of something he had been conscious of from the first—the strangest thing in his little friend's large little composition,

a temper, a sensibility, even a private ideal, which made him as privately disown the stuff his people were made of.

This shows that children could think of disowning parents. We can presume that Morgan at this time is eleven or twelve, maybe younger. Then we have something about the gradations of knowledge. This is said of Pemberton:

> When he tried to figure to himself the morning twilight of childhood, so as to deal with it safely, he saw it was never fixed, never arrested, that ignorance, at the instant he touched it, was already flushing faintly into knowledge, that there was nothing that at a given moment you could say an intelligent child didn't know. It seemed to him that he himself knew too much to imagine Morgan's simplicity and too little to disembroil his tangle.

So there was a lot of knowledge, and not enough.

Then some of the words that are used as representing evil in *The Turn of the Screw*, "lying" and "cheating," are used here too:

> "You're right. Don't worry them," Pemberton pursued. "Except for that, they *are* charming people."
>
> "Except for *their* lying and *their* cheating?"
>
> "I say—I say!" cried Pemberton, imitating a little tone of the lad's which was itself an imitation.

Morgan is aware that his parents use other people badly and are also used badly:

> "And what good does it do? Haven't I seen the way people treat them—the 'nice' people, the ones they want to know? They'll take anything from them—they'll lie down and be trampled on. The nice ones hate that—they just sicken them. You're the only really nice person we know."

They have it out. Morgan has said plainly that's what he thinks about his parents, and Pemberton is a little shocked, but things go on.

Morgan walked on and after a little had begun again: "Well, now that you know I know and that we look at the facts and keep nothing back—it's much more comfortable, isn't it?"

"My dear boy, it's so amusing, so interesting, that it will surely be quite impossible for me to forego such hours as these."

This made Morgan stop once more. "You *do* keep something back. Oh you're not straight—I am!"

"How am I not straight?"

"Oh you've got your idea!"

"My idea?"

"Why that I probably shan't make old—make older—bones, and that you can stick it out till I'm removed."

Pemberton is concerned about Morgan: he is a sick boy and he may die any time.

"You *are* too clever to live!" Pemberton repeated.

"I call it a mean idea," Morgan pursued. "But I shall punish you by the way I hang on."

"Look out or I'll poison you!" Pemberton laughed.

"I'm stronger and better every year. Haven't you noticed that there hasn't been a doctor near me since you came?"

"*I'm* your doctor," said the young man, taking his arm and drawing him tenderly on again.

Morgan proceeded and after a few steps gave a sigh of mingled weariness and relief. "Ah now that we look at the facts it's all right!"

        ❧   ❧   ❧   ❧

Morgan had a romantic imagination, fed by poetry and history, and he would have liked those who "bore his name"—as he used to say to Pemberton with the humour that made his queer delicacies manly—to carry themselves with an air.

We can imagine a child saying, "I'd like the people who bear my name to carry themselves better." People would think no child could say it, but James says a child does. Morgan wants his parents to live up to what *he* is. This feeling hasn't been articulated, but many children have had it.

"The Pupil" is not as good as *The Turn of the Screw,* but it is one of the stories that helps to explain *The Turn of the Screw.* James was going after something in the ethical field all the time. He did not articulate it very plainly, but in *The Turn of the Screw,* the deepest feeling of it is to be had, because there it is related to some of the eternal things. The supernatural is a means of making *The Turn of the Screw* a source story, something beyond the earth (the unearthly is part of the earth: it helps to explain it). And so, through the unearthly, a dimension is given to the ethical problem as we see it in "The Pupil" and many other places, that it doesn't have often in those other places. We should, in looking at "The Pupil," ask why something comes over in *The Turn of the Screw* in a *gnawing* way, in a usefully tormenting way, that doesn't come over in the other stories, though certainly the other stories can be effective.

2

Governess as God's Spy

THE FACT that Henry James has taken people so much these days is important, and one of the things it tends to show is that people are looking to be "saved"—that is, they'd like to be able to look at themselves and feel that they are worthy of being and worthy of going on. I talk this way, somewhat theologically, because one of the things in Henry James is the awareness of his father, Henry James, Sr., who was very theological, very deep, and an important mind in his own right. He was very much given to the study of the person in relation to God, and to the study of good and evil in ways that are taking on more currency now.

To say that Henry James wanted to be "good" seems to be very strange. That the most sophisticated writer of this century, as some have said—that his desire should have been to be *good,* seems infantine. But nonetheless, it is so. One of the things Aesthetic Realism is trying to make clear is that you cannot be good unless you have an awareness of evil, and that awareness doesn't make any sense until you see an aesthetic relation between the two.

James has said quite often, as his father did, that goodness arises from aesthetics (and one can say that aesthetics arises from goodness). The fact that something which is beautiful is associated with evil, unless that beauty is entire, is one of the things we can see in *The Turn of the Screw*. There are these beautiful children who also are evil. But the relation of sweetness and cruelty, good and evil, is in James's work generally, including his critical work.

It was felt for a long while that because James writes so much about elegant interiors, and so much about tables with tea things on them, that he was a finicky person—without its being seen what the finickiness went for. The finickiness went essentially for this: that you praise God by seeing him in detail; that as soon as you get a hurried, indefinite view of God, you are insulting whatever he may be. James, then, wanted to show the deep meaning of what may seem inconsequential to others. He felt that to have a passion for life is to have a passion for its details.

One of the things we notice about James is that when he talked, there was an attempt to be exact, but there was something rolling. There are quite a few reports of his conversation, and they are all pretty interesting. When people write about James, they suddenly take on a lift. There is something written about him by E. F. Benson in an autobiographical work called *As We Were*. Benson was the son of the archbishop from whom, it is said, James got the idea of *The Turn of the Screw*.

First Benson talks about the fact that James would deal with the most trivial things as if they were tremendously important. In his work, there is a desire to make the unseen, the untouched as if it were existent. And he felt that the worship of God was to see a little thing as if it mattered. He could talk about the slightest thing as if it were epochal and profound; and it seemed very funny. Then he liked to get vague about definite things—everyone knew what it was, but he'd be vague anyway. Benson says:

> The most trivial incident thus became something rich and sumptuous with the hints of this cumulative treatment. I remember, as the simplest instance, how he described a call he paid at dusk on some neighbours at Rye, how he rang the bell and nothing happened, how he rang again and again waited, how at the end there came steps in the passage and the door was slowly opened, and there appeared in advance on the threshold, "something black, something canine." To have said a black dog, would not have done at all: he eschewed all such bald statements in these entrancing narrations, during which he involved himself in enormous and complicated sentences, all rolling and sonorous to the ear, as if he was composing aloud.

But the sentences were rolling and exact. Here is another description:

> It took a long time to arrive at that succinct statement, but the progress toward it, though abandoned, was like some adventure in a gorgeous jungle, a tropical forest of interlaced verbiage. All other talk, when he was of the company, seemed thin and jejune by this elaborate discourse, to which one listened entranced by its humours and its decorations.

This manner came from the deep desire to give a thing profundity and give it all its detail: to make sure nothing that it had was disregarded.

The desire too was to present the ordinary as if it were infinite. This is the manner of art.

Getting now to *The Turn of the Screw*. There is an anthology called *The Story*, edited by Mark Schorer, which has *The Turn of the Screw* in it and the part of

James's preface which deals with it, and then an essay by Edmund Wilson, and another essay by Robert Heilman.

Now, the essay by Wilson was written in 1934 and then very gingerly revised a little in 1948. Even without Freud's interference, Edmund Wilson, I suppose, could not see straight now and then; but the combination of Freud *and* Wilson is gigantic. However, it represents a point of view which has been quite popular: that the governess was endowed with a whole bunch of sexual repressions, and she was hungering for the guardian of the two children, and because of her repressions she made up this story, and in fact there were no apparitions, ghosts, spirits, spectres, but they came out of her neurotic, insufficiently courageous sexual disposition.

The other essay is by Robert Heilman; it is fourteen years later (1948), and appeared in *The University of Kansas City Review*. Heilman mentions original sin as something seen in *The Turn of the Screw* by Katherine Anne Porter, one of the most renowned of American short story writers. Heilman's essay is a pretty remarkable thing. He is a person who is not afraid to deal with theology as if it had some use. However, Heilman does not want to see the children as evil as such. It seems that people are afraid of their childhood.

Evil doesn't begin at the age of thirteen, it begins in a pure form as soon as a person has the chance to make a choice, as soon as he has a chance to look around and see what's what and what he can get out of it. Evil then is in operation.

The notion of evil that Aesthetic Realism has is the notion of evil that Henry James somewhat had: it is the notion of people in the process of being themselves, being unjust to what is not themselves. Injustice is evil.

If you affirm, maintain, please yourself by being unjust in any form whatsoever to what is not yourself, the evil that was in you is in operation; and no matter what age.

One of the most important things quoted by Leon Edel, one of the principal editors of James, is a statement of James about the Oscar Wilde trial. Now Oscar Wilde is not, as no one has been, an exemplar of total virtue; yet I think he is better than most people, all in all. It is a pity that his wickedness should take such an exotic form. James was interested in the Wilde matter, and Edel quotes a letter written just before he was to write *The Turn of the Screw*. This is how James talks about children. Edel says:

> In a letter to Edmund Gosse, while the trial was in progress, James alluded to the . . . "little beasts of witnesses. What a nest of almost infant blackmailing!"

People have known of such things all the time, but the idea that the children in *The Turn of the Screw*, because they look angelic, could have evil in them as such—this simply doesn't come to people's minds. They know the things that have been said, but they are afraid to see it.

Children are very diverse, but they have been seen as either "naughty" or "brats," or as very good. The same mother who will go after a child and condemn the child and raise her voice, will talk about the innocence of children: "Of course he's only a child, you know." Persons after they've grown up also have a big fear of seeing themselves as children. They know they were children, they know there were days in childhood, but they don't want to look at them. Somehow, there is a break.

And in the meantime, the physician from Vienna kind of muddied the waters.

I think Edmund Wilson is afraid to look at himself as a child; I think most literary people right now in America are. I think Thomas Wolfe, with all his autobiography, was afraid. I think even Miss Carson McCullers, who writes about children so poignantly, is also a little afraid. It is very difficult to accept what we don't remember, and it is very difficult to think that the drama of good and bad was in us.

James uses the word *plasticity* about the children. Now, plasticity means the being able to be molded; but it doesn't mean that the person who is molded doesn't do a little molding on his own. There is no denying that children are plastic, but the question is, do they use plasticity on others? For example, have you ever seen a child go into a confectionary store and prove to the man who has the store that because he's so nice he should get three candies without paying, or that his mother will pay? I call that the plastic effect of children on confectionary owners.

One of the things that has been left out in the excoriations of the governess is the question: Do children not only undergo evil, but do they make for evil? I think that they do, and that the possibility of evil, once it is aroused, goes on affecting others. If this is so, then it is not right to deal with children as if they were only plastic.

Is it possible for children to go after power?—that is the important thing. And this is the one thing I haven't seen taken up in the writings that tend to disparage the governess: Are children as young as Miles and Flora capable of going after power? I think they are, and it is something that the writers and artists of America do not want to see. They will talk of how parents tended to hurt *them*—a great deal of that has been done; but how, between the ages of two and twelve, they wanted to manage their parents or other adults, and did use various cunning, conquering ways—that is something which people are afraid to think about.

When does the desire for power begin? Does it begin as soon as you vote? And if people vote at eighteen, does it begin then? Do children go after power? When? How does it show itself? Do they have a feeling of victory over others? Do they get a pleasure in thinking other people are in an inferior position? We know that children will laugh if a person slips on the pavement; we know they will laugh if a person looks ridiculous. But when does the desire for power begin?

The possibility of going after power Aesthetic Realism sees as in everyone. We know that children will try to have power over cats; we know they will try to have power over dogs, and occasionally they get bitten by dogs; we know they try to have power over other children, and there's a row. Do they stop there, or would they like to have power over everybody, including adults—their parents in particular?

The essential thing that hasn't been said elsewhere and is said by Aesthetic Realism is that Miles and Flora were after a certain kind of power. Perhaps they were encouraged to go after this power by Quint and Jessel. That may be true, just as a man can be encouraged to become a wily politician; but the fact is, that when encouraged he goes after the power.

Somehow we know that adults are after power. We feel that every adult we know, perhaps, is after power.

But when did it begin? Just what day did it begin? What is the age — seventeen, nineteen, twenty-one, eleven, fourteen? Do you get it at puberty? When does it begin? That is the question which I'd like people to think about. It is a question that thinking America and critical America is afraid of, because it would mean that maybe we were conceited persons at the age of four, maybe we were after power.

Now lying, which children can do, is next to pretending; pretending is next to hiding. Once we lie, we are trying to take advantage of people. Taking advantage of people has many forms, including the form which has gone on in history of using them for our financial advantage. I have seen autobiographies of people who have been quite acquisitive. I remember some in a book by Forbes, *Men Who Make Our Nation*. They own a great deal, they own all kinds of clay factories, tin factories in Ohio, asbestos factories in Indiana, roller-bearing factories in Illinois—they own, they own, they own. And they all have autobiographies in which they were going back to their childhood and pining for the Old Swimming Hole. Here they were, with stocks, they were directors, and they were ready to put aside their debentures, their stocks, their bonds, their real estate titles—all to go back to the dear Swimming Hole. And I say that the things that made them later own so much in the roller-bearing way or the oil-cloth way or the clay way (one of them seemed to own all of Xenia, Ohio)—that was beginning at the time of the dear Old Swimming Hole.

Children, it is known, can be very wily. Every eighth child is called by other children "Stinky"; and there are other names used. Children know. And there are names, the mild form of which is Sneaky. What does that come from?

I am now going to present some passages, which tend to explain the story of *The Turn of the Screw* and, I think, help sustain the Aesthetic Realism point of view.

Edel is contradictory. Though he doesn't go along with the Edmund Wilson idea that the governess is really the bad person, that she was bringing her neuroticism to the Bly estate, making up these ghosts, yet he doesn't want to go so far as to say that the children themselves were bad. And James in a way doesn't do this either: he is ambiguous.

The nearest that James has said about the children being evil is in his *Notebooks,* and it seems Wilson hadn't read the *Notebooks* at the time he made his statements. We find in James's *Notebooks* the following:

> The servants, wicked and depraved, corrupt and deprave the children; the children are bad, full of evil, to a sinister degree.

There is a semi-colon; do you want to say the children are bad because of the servants, or that they are bad anyway? James is ambiguous; I don't think he wholly saw. His statements about *The Turn of the Screw* are somewhat contradictory. Leon Edel tells us this:

> One evening in 1913 (so the anecdote goes) Henry James and his compatriot John Singer Sargent, who had lately painted James's portrait, dined at a great old London house at No. 3 Cumberland Place. The conversation turned, at one moment during the evening, to ghosts and tales of horror, and Mildred, Lady Gosford (at the home of whose parents the dinner was taking place) told the novelist that she had read *The Turn of the Screw* with excitement and a mounting sense of terror—without fully understanding what was happening. The novelist, speaking slowly and quietly, said: "My dear Mildred, no more do I. The story was told me by Archbishop Benson.

I have caught the impression his mystery made on me and I have passed it on to you—but as to understanding it, it is just gleams and glooms."

He knew he was dealing with something that wasn't just contrived. James knew, though at times he was very jaunty, that in *The Turn of the Screw* he had reached a fundamental something. Edel says:

William Lyon Phelps has quoted James as saying "I meant to scare the whole world with that story."

Then in his preface James calls it an *"amusette"*— a thing to amuse. Which shows that James didn't wholly see what he was doing.

James doesn't want to say everything, even if he could; because to say that the children are given to various malpractices of the sort that have got into the books, to get to the details would spoil his purpose. People want to talk about such awful things as carnal pleasure, but they don't want to talk about evil straight. Evil as such is deeper and more terrible than carnal pleasure. That is why the persons who have tried to explain *The Turn of the Screw* in terms of a sexually incomplete governess and maybe two sexually aware children, are really treacherous to James. James is trying to show the evil which is *beneath* these things. The evil beneath stealing is more terrible than the stealing; the evil beneath a lie is more terrible than the lie; the evil beneath what the YMCA would call self-pollution is more terrible than the self-pollution; the evil beneath using a person inconsiderately and libidinously is more terrible than the successful libidinousness.

And so James wants to present things hintingly. There is a lot of what Mr. Fenimore Cooper would call well-placed crackling of leaves—because the leaves show what the forest can mean, as they rustle mysteriously.

The title of *The Turn of the Screw* has engaged people. It could have various meanings: the motion of a screw, the circumference changing to center, the sense of a circle whirling to a center. There is the quietness of the motion; the stealthiness, in a sense. I remember a person saying that whenever he put a screw into wood, he felt as if he were doing something awfully devilish.

Then there is a relation between the motion of a screw and the way a worm eats an apple. But there is also a sense of looseness and tightness. All these things interested James: he was very much interested by the mechanical.

If someone has a dream in which a nail goes into wood, one of the enthusiastic men given to Freud could say, "Well, you see what that dream means—and your mother was there?—well, very simple indeed. You are trying to be sadistic and also trying to take over your mother from somebody else." But Aesthetic Realism says that the motion of anything into anything—the motion, let us say, of a raindrop into a pool—occurred before people were, and it is deeper. Sex is an example of something central meeting something perhaps less central— or whatever you want to call it. But it would be a superficialization of reality to say that sex explains these things. These things explain sex. And that is the way James saw it. Sex is an example of people becoming one, but the becoming one of things occurred before sex was talked about.

The attitude of the man of Vienna to literature was superficial and vulgar, in the Jamesian sense—because it was too easy. James very often uses the word "vulgar" for people who want to get opinions without thinking.

So the meaning of the title is important. There is a phrase very famous in French literature: "*C'est Vénus tout entière à sa proie attachée.*" It is from Racine's *Phèdre*. In English it would be: "It is Venus, all of her, joined to her prey." It is very musical in the French. But the idea of people coming together and not being in a good relation, is terrible.

James was constantly taken by the problem of appearance and reality. In his stories very often there are ladies who look very good, but who are entrancing and hollow. You don't see the hollowness right away.

The question of what a thing is and how it seems interested James very much. If you see the pictures of every person who later came to be a cut-throat, a faker, a sadist, a person not giving a damn for others—every one of them between the ages of one and five could look somewhat innocent. If you don't believe me, study any album whatsoever. There isn't a liar, faker, killer, bomb-thrower, well-poisoner, cattle-rustler, horsethief, loanshark, who as a child didn't have a look of innocence. Go to any album. It is really terrible: how can these sweet little things, these toothsome humans, these ravishing little beings—how can they come to be loansharks and killers?

The problem of appearance and reality is important. We know how it is used in certain Westerns: a blonde looking as innocent as anything comes up to the hero, but she's really a plant by the villain.

Yet the beauty of the children in this story is something insisted on. The governess, when she comes to Bly, sees beauty of a sort she hasn't seen before. She says about Flora:

> She was the most beautiful child I had ever seen, and I afterwards wondered that my employer had not told me more of her.

NOTE: This quotation is from the first section of the governess' narrative. I summarize the main events in the story leading up to what we are approaching.

The governess has been hired by the handsome uncle of the children in London, and has come to the country estate called Bly, a very nice place, and has begun to instruct Flora, a most beautiful and amiable child. The first hint that things are not as good as they seem is when she receives a letter from the school where the boy Miles is. He is being sent home: expelled; but they don't say why. The governess is uneasy, and thinks perhaps he did something wicked. She consults with the housekeeper, Mrs. Grose, and Mrs. Grose assures her that Miles is as good as he is beautiful and he could not possibly have done anything justifying his expulsion from anywhere. When the governess meets Miles, she is charmed by him. She agrees with Mrs. Grose and decides to say nothing about the letter from the school. Miles doesn't say anything either.

It is shortly after this that the governess sees the ghost of Peter Quint. At first she thinks it is a strange man prowling about the place, but when she describes him to Mrs. Grose, Mrs. Grose identifies him as Quint, the uncle's former valet, now dead.

The governess decides not to say anything about this either. In the first place, she can't prove it and it would make her look queer; in the second place, the one condition the uncle laid down on giving her the job was that she not bother him for any reason whatsoever. She does not think the apparition is a threat to her, but feels she should protect the children from him. She doesn't know why.

She teaches both the children, and with all her cares, finds comfort in their company. They mix learning with games, and she is now by the lake with Flora, pretending she is something or other, as part of Flora's game. This is the scene in which she sees the ghost of Miss Jessel for the first time and is convinced that Flora sees her too, and pretends not to.
—*Ed.*

The governess, like everyone else, is in a puzzling interaction between high and low. Nobody has yet thought he wasn't higher than something and lower than something. The governess is in a pretty distinguished position, but then there are persons higher. She says:

> . . . and that was merely, thanks to my superior, my exalted stamp, a happy and highly distinguished sinecure. I forget what I was on the present occasion; I only remember that I was something very important and very quiet and that Flora was playing very hard. We were on the edge of the lake, and, as we had lately begun geography, the lake was the Sea of Azof.

She is teaching, and teachers have been low, but they have also been high. She is teaching geography, and so the lake (which comes in later) is called the Sea of Azof.

The next thing I see of importance in the phraseology is as to the shade and heat. As I have said, coolness and heat is something James is very fond of dealing with; he sees a great deal of meaning in it. People can go through life without deciding whether they want to be hot or cold. We have an idiom, "he's blowing hot and cold"; and people spend lifetimes blowing hot and cold. This means a great deal in ever so many fields. So James is fond of presenting shade that is heat and heat that is shade; and he does it very well.

> The old trees, the thick shrubbery, made a great and pleasant shade, but it was all suffused with the brightness of the hot, still hour. There was no ambiguity in anything; none whatever, at least, in the conviction I from one moment to another found myself forming as to what I should see straight before me and across the lake as a consequence of raising my eyes.

There is a good deal about raising one's eyes here. There are two ways of seeing: one is to raise one's eyes, and the other is to look inward; and there is a relation between the two. Miss Jessel, when she is described, is very often with head bent down; and the governess very often has to decide whether she is going to raise her eyes or not. This does occur sometimes in the idea of terror: what will you see if you raise your eyes? If you have your head bowed, you can get by, but if you raise your eyes, what *will* you see? The governess feels that she might be seeing something that perhaps it is not comfortable to see.

Proceeding with this section. Flora is playing now, and the governess wonders what Flora sees and what she doesn't see. And Flora, being a very adept little lass, can hide what she sees and doesn't see. She is very good at that. She's been taught by experts.

My heart had stood still for an instant with the wonder
and terror of the question whether she too would see; and
I held my breath while I waited for what a cry from her,
what some sudden innocent sign either of interest or of
alarm, would tell me. I waited, but nothing came; then,
in the first place—and there is something more dire in
this, I feel, than in anything I have to relate—I was determined by a sense that, within a minute, all sounds from
her had previously dropped; and, in the second, by the
circumstance that, also within the minute, she had, in
her play, turned her back to the water. This was her
attitude when I at last looked at her—looked with the
confirmed conviction that we were still, together, under
direct personal notice. She had picked up a small flat piece
of wood, which happened to have in it a little hole that had
evidently suggested to her the idea of sticking in another
fragment that might figure as a mast and make the thing
a boat. This second morsel, as I watched her, she was
very markedly and intently attempting to tighten in its
place. My apprehension of what she was doing sustained
me so that after some seconds I felt I was ready for more.
Then I again shifted my eyes—I faced what I had to face.

This is an important passage. The governess is watching Flora see something or not see something, and
she suspects that Flora is seeing the desired Miss Jessel.
This is told in a very taking and quiet way. James's
style at its best is smooth and sudden and unexpected
—that is, it glides along, but there is a quality that
makes for a little breathlessness.

When a child seems to be going through something
big and doesn't seem to do what other children do—
either cry, or say ooh, or gasp, or something of the kind
—then mothers can get worried. One of the signs of
illness that a mother sees is when a child doesn't go
through some of the customary expressions of delight or
disappointment, like or dislike. A child gets into the
state which adults can get into: "Nothing means any-

thing to me, bring on your terrors, bring on your
ecstasies, see if I care." But when we see that in a child
as such, it is very ugly. When people meet something
they should be moved by, and they have got the art
of not showing that they are moved, it isn't very good
to see. Sometimes—to pun about it—the soundless is
unsound.

Now, one of the reasons I feel that Flora is presented
here as unattractive, is that she has such control of herself, she doesn't do those things children ordinarily do:
"Oh, look! Look what I saw! Look at this! Isn't this nice?
Oh, come here, I've got to show you this!" Sometimes
that is annoying, children saying "Come here" so often;
but the other thing is even more annoying: there is a
kind of monopolistic, secret contempt. Flora seems to
have that.—So we have:

> I waited for what a cry from her, what some sudden in-
> nocent sign either of interest or of alarm, would tell me.
> . . . All sounds from her had previously dropped; and
> . . . also within the minute, she had, in her play, turned
> her back to the water.

Now this may have symbolism, of course, but that it
is necessarily sexual symbolism is untrue. Having one's
back to the water can be seen as simple disdain. Water
has been seen as holy, or as that through which a person finds holiness: that is why a person is baptized with
water. So Flora turns her back to the water. Then the
governess says:

> We were still, together, under direct personal notice.

That means that Miss Jessel is around and she is looking at what's going on.

And then this passage that so much has been made of. The flurry of making so much of this is one of the most foolish things in American criticism. When the history of American criticism is written, there will be some foolish things in it—some of the foolish things will be statements about Whitman; but one of the foolish things is the great flurry about why Flora was picking up this small flat piece of wood.

> She had picked up a small flat piece of wood, which happened to have in it a little hole that had evidently suggested to her the idea of sticking in another fragment that might figure as a mast and make the thing a boat.

Now, it happens that all children like to get things together. The joining of things—all joining is like sex, that's all there is to it. I suppose we'd better abolish joining. For instance, there are certain chairs at Macy's —they used to give them to you in parts, and you'd put the parts together. I guess that would mean a terrific orgy. Not that it doesn't have a meaning, but sex is an example of it. The idea of two things coming together existed before sex. If one wants to say that every time an Indian used to make fire—and the way the Indians made fire looks very obscene—he was sublimating, one can; but I believe the Indians got fire because they wanted fire, not because they were looking for "substitutes."

What I see this passage about Flora as meaning is that one person can see herself as capturing another person. Sex is a kind of capturing, that is true. Two things are joined. But the idea of joining is a larger idea than sex. The fact that the atoms do stick together doesn't mean that they're all lewd, nor that the molecules are lewd. But there are some kinds of getting

together that, quite obviously, are not as good as others.
One can say that this is an idea of "I have you and you
have me"; and if one wants to say there is sex there, very
well. I don't see it as necessary.

> This second morsel, as I watched her, she was very
> markedly and intently attempting to tighten in its place.

There is some intensity and concentration here, and
what James is saying is that Flora is more and more
trying to establish a hold and make sure that her conquest is complete. She wants to have something utterly.

The other strange thing is this: that if Flora is going
after Miss Jessel, it seems to me if she were a little
Lesbian, this particular symbol would not be the proper
one. One of the strangest things is that the girl should
have gone after Miss Jessel and the boy after Peter
Quint. If it were just sex, I don't see the necessity for
that. Not that it couldn't be, but I don't see the necessity for the symbol anyway. I think that one of these
days, when the curiosities of later American criticisms
are being assessed and studied, this pother about the
symbol of the bits of wood will get in.

We are now at Section 7. The sense of trembling
between two worlds, between certainty and uncertainty,
is always maintained. Uncertainty and certainty are essential in drama. As Hamlet says, "To be or not to be,"
the governess is asking, "To believe what I see or not to
believe what I see?" She is in a state of uncertainty.
There is a flutter of hell and heaven all through the
work.—Section 7 begins this way:

> I got hold of Mrs. Grose as soon after this as I could:
> and I can give no intelligible account of how I fought out

the interval. Yet I still hear myself cry as I fairly threw myself into her arms: "They *know* — it's too monstrous; they know, they know!"

"And what on earth—?" I felt her incredulity as she held me.

"Why, all that *we* know—and heaven knows what else besides!"

This is presented in such an uncertain way that we can feel the narrator is trying to be exact. How much does a child know in its way? We know that a child can know good things that an adult might not—that is in the phrase, "And a little child shall lead them." As to the other thing, how much a child knows of evil, much could be said too. Assuming that the child has immediately come from that universal factory where both evil and good are, she has them both very freshly and working with great gusto, in a way. At any rate, a child can be knowing. "Knowingness" is one of the things we associate with children. It's not just knowing, it is knowing and acting as if you don't. When children don't want to answer, the mothers feel that. The child just blandly says, "No, mother, how could I be there?" This doesn't have to do with all evil, but a child can very blandly say, "I wasn't there at all. Why don't you ask somebody else?" Mothers have experienced this a great deal. The being able to tell a fib with some sort of smoothness, is a talent that hardly any child doesn't have.

Then there is something about Flora's keeping things to herself. We see that phrase very often in *What Maisie Knew*. Maisie feels she has a right to keep things to herself.—Mrs. Grose has just been told that Flora saw. The governess says:

Mrs. Grose took it as she might have taken a blow in the stomach. "She has told you?" she panted.

"Not a word—that's the horror. She kept it to herself! The child of eight, *that* child!" Unutterable still, for me, was the stupefaction of it.

We have two problems here. Could children see something and know something which they wouldn't want to tell? I think yes. Of course, if you want to say children don't see ghosts—all right, I agree to that. But that children can be aware something is pleasing them and that there is something to go for, and they wouldn't tell—I think that is so.

The governess describes what she saw:

"Another person—this time; but a figure of quite as unmistakable horror and evil: a woman in black, pale and dreadful—with such an air also, and such a face!—on the other side of the lake. I was there with the child—quiet for the hour; and in the midst of it she came."

Then Mrs. Grose asks:

"Was she someone you've never seen?"

"Yes. But someone the child has. Someone *you* have." Then, to show how I had thought it all out: "My predecessor—the one who died."

"Miss Jessel?"

"Miss Jessel. You don't believe me?" I pressed.

She turned right and left in her distress. "How can you be sure?"

This drew from me, in the state of my nerves, a flash of impatience. "Then ask Flora—*she's* sure!" But I had no sooner spoken than I caught myself up. "No, for God's sake, *don't!* She'll say she isn't—she'll lie!"

Mrs. Grose was not too bewildered instinctively to protest. "Ah, how *can* you?"

"Because I'm clear. Flora doesn't want me to know."

"It's only then to spare you."

"No, no—there are depths, depths! The more I go over it, the more I see in it, and the more I see in it the more I fear. I don't know what I *don't* see—what I *don't* fear!"

This is important, because if the governess is bent on persecuting Flora and making her out a liar, then of course she is an awful person. If this were so, one would have to ask, what motive is there? Assuming the governess is interested in the uncle, would she make her point by maligning the niece and the nephew? I do not see it. To be able to say to the uncle: "Look, Flora is so bad and Miles is so bad"—I do not see where the uncle would be so impressed as to look on the governess more favorably.

The way this is told is pretty authentic. You can't prove anything like this—if a person doesn't want to say she has seen something. So the governess says, about Flora: "No, for God's sake, don't! She'll say she isn't— she'll lie!" And: "No, no—there are depths, depths!" And what are these depths? This is what I'm trying to answer.

The implication is that James felt that he as a child and others as children could use the persons about them in a way that was evil purely. It is the way I have talked about a good deal. It is a way that says: "A person made by God exists for me to have glory." This glory is based on what can be called ill will or contempt, and it is evil pure. Because as soon as we begin using the weakness of another with the hope that the person continues weak or foolish to maintain our own glory—there is nothing more ugly in this world. Since this is so much a part of Aesthetic Realism ethics—the saying that this is where we start being thieves and villains and scound-

rels and rogues—and since it begins in this insidious
subtle way, and since *The Turn of the Screw* is one of
the very few works that deals with it centrally, it is important to understand it.

The "depths" are the depths of evil, where the world
is used for one's glory—the world as represented by two
servants, the lady and the man. And once people start
using each other for evil, they cannot stop. This is implied in some of Swedenborg's descriptions of hell and
the bad spirits consorting with each other. As soon as
it is found that because of our freedom, as a theologian
would say, we have the possibility of despising what is
around us—the beginning of evil has been. The evil
itself is the separation. The second step is using separation for conceit and contempt. That is what the children have done, Flora before the age of eight, and Miles
before his age.

This is what is important to see, because the "depths"
that James didn't see clearly and the governess didn't
see clearly, are either that, or, the question is—what are
they? I don't believe the governess would say, "There
are depths, depths!" if there were something sexual going on, though this is a Victorian time. After all, the
Victorian farms had all kinds of things like that going
on. One would say, "Oh, the ugliness of it," but not
"the depths"—that is too big a word. It is the relation
of self to self that has come in.

According to Aesthetic Realism, the greatest sin that
a person can have is the desire for contempt. Because as
soon as you have contempt, as soon as you don't want
to see another person as having the fulness that you
have, you can rob that person, hurt that person, kill that
person. These three things come out of the insufficient
awareness of another person or another thing.

This is what the children are doing: they are caught in their contempt procedure. Contempt with something that looks like love is a combination that many people have.

We'll look at the text further.

Miss Jessel is described as sad. She doesn't seem to be having a wonderful time. However she is also described by the governess as very bad:

> "For the woman's a horror of horrors."
>
> Mrs. Grose, at this, fixed her eyes a minute on the ground; then at last raising them, "Tell me how you know," she said.
>
> "Then you admit it's what she was?" I cried.
>
> "Tell me how you know," my friend simply repeated.
>
> "Know? By seeing her! By the way she looked."
>
> "At you, do you mean—so wickedly?"
>
> "Dear me, no—I could have borne that. She gave me never a glance. She only fixed the child."
>
> Mrs. Grose tried to see it. "Fixed her?"
>
> "Ah, with such awful eyes!"
>
> She stared at mine as if they might really have resembled them. "Do you mean of dislike?"
>
> "God help us, no. Of something much worse."
>
> "Worse than dislike?"—this left her indeed at a loss.
>
> "With a determination—indescribable. With a kind of fury of intention."
>
> I made her turn pale. "Intention?"
>
> "To get hold of her." Mrs. Grose—her eyes just lingering on mine—gave a shudder and walked to the window; and while she stood there looking out I completed my statement. "*That's* what Flora knows."

This is an important passage. There is the word *fixed*, which can be seen in relation to the title. The notion of people "fixing" another or joining another, taking over another, is deeper than the idea of sex. Miss Jessel is

said to have "fixed the child." But Flora apparently is
going after a little fixing of her own—with that much
talked about symbol of the two bits of wood. There is
a certain pleasure that children can get in sometimes
fixing a poor fly or a butterfly, impaling it. And it has
to do with the sense of victory. Now out of that can be
the idea of sex, certainly; but what I'm trying to get at
is that sex is one example of the possible bad use of one
person by another.

"For the woman's a horror of horrors." That is intense.
"She only fixed the child . . . Ah, with such awful
eyes!" Here there isn't anything too terrible. Sometimes
we do that: we feel someone has done us wrong, and
we give a look. Sometimes when people are led away to
jail they give a look at the witness, if they can; they try
to pierce him with a look. Miss Jessel could be doing a
little fixing, or trying to, because she's also sad. And she
has awful eyes. The governess says Mrs. Grose "stared
at mine as if they might really have resembled them"—
this is the governess being quite sensible, seeing that
this quality of Miss Jessel could be in her. Any virtuous
person will admit the possibility of all evil: if you don't
admit the possibility of evil in you, you can hardly be
virtuous. So the governess is having a time, and she
shows it by saying that her eyes could look like Miss
Jessel's.

"With a determination—indescribable. With a kind
of fury of intention." The thing that we get in Flora's
dealing with the wood is also determination. So they
both have determination.

"To get hold of her." That sometimes means punish-
ing: "Oh, if I ever get hold of her!" But they are punish-
ing each other while they need each other. *"That's* what
Flora˙ knows." And Flora seems more composed than
Miss Jessel.

Mrs. Grose says:

> "The person was in black, you say?"
> "In mourning—rather poor, almost shabby. But—yes—
> with extraordinary beauty." I now recognized to what I
> had at last, stroke by stroke, brought the victim of my
> confidence, for she quite visibly weighed this. "Oh, hand-
> some—very, very," I insisted: "wonderfully handsome.
> But infamous."

So Miss Jessel is in black and she is dressed poorly,
but there is something distinguished about her. She
reminds one of those ladies who dress in black and one
can see they don't have too much money, but still they
look genteel.

> She slowly came back to me. "Miss Jessel—*was* in-
> famous." She once more took my hand in both her own,
> holding it as tight as if to fortify me against the increase
> of alarm I might draw from this disclosure. "They were
> both infamous," she finally said.

The strange thing is the implication that Miss Jessel
was very close to Quint, and yet she was close to Flora
too. That has to be explained. One can only do it by
surmise.

The being infamous seems to have to do with the
Quint relation, but the implication that there is something deeper here shows that the actual thing was the
having of another person.

What does it mean for someone to give up his soul?
We can see that as a big thing in the Faust stories and
plays, and elsewhere. What does it mean? The idea is
that in letting another person be very nice to you and
giving you your way, you lose your soul in a certain

specific fashion. Faustus says, "I'll give up my soul if you let me have my way."

But Miss Jessel, even so, is troubled. Whenever we see her, she seems to be in a state of dark repentance, though she has to go on. She's like a cork in a torrent; the cork is sorry to be in the torrent, but it has to go on.

Mrs. Grose says about Miss Jessel:

"Poor woman—she paid for it!"

Mrs. Grose shows sympathy for Miss Jessel, which means that Miss Jessel, though she was after something, was also sad, both in the relation with Quint and in the relation with Flora, by implication.

A little later, James once more writes about the relation of innocence to evil. In the same way as a skin disease sometimes has a most lovely color, so there can be some beautiful visual effects that attend the undesirable. And James isn't tired, in this story, of bringing out this paradox. The governess is talking about Flora:

> To gaze into the depths of blue of the child's eyes and pronounce their loveliness a trick of premature cunning was to be guilty of a cynicism in preference to which I naturally preferred to abjure my judgment and, so far as might be, my agitation. I couldn't abjure for merely wanting to, but I could repeat to Mrs. Grose—as I did there, over and over, in the small hours—that with their voices in the air, their pressure on one's heart and their fragrant faces against one's cheek, everything fell to the ground but their incapacity and their beauty. It was a pity that, somehow, to settle this once for all, I had equally to re-enumerate the signs of subtlety that, in the afternoon, by the lake, had made a miracle of my show of self-possession.

The whole story is written as if the narrator was not
ready to believe something but is compelled to believe
it. There is a tentativeness, there is a putting aside of the
screen bit by bit. And the narrator is ashamed somewhat
that she is compelled to see this. Technically, James is
very good when he describes the increasing certitude,
the growing lucidity. It is done very well.

Now Mrs. Grose tells the governess about the relation
of Miles and the two of the house, Quint and Jessel. The
governess says:

What my friend had had in mind proved to be im-
mensely to the purpose. It was neither more nor less than
the circumstances that for a period of several months
Quint and the boy had been perpetually together. It was
in fact the very appropriate truth that she [Mrs. Grose]
had ventured to criticize the propriety, to hint at the in-
congruity, of so close an alliance, and even to go so far
on the subject as a frank overture to Miss Jessel. Miss
Jessel had, with a most strange manner, requested her to
mind her business, and the good woman had, on this,
directly approached little Miles. What she had said to
him, since I pressed, was that *she* liked to see young
gentlemen not forget their station.

I pressed again, of course, at this. "You reminded him
that Quint was only a base menial?"

"As you might say! And it was his answer, for one
thing, that was bad."

"And for another thing?" I waited. "He repeated your
words to Quint?"

"No, not that. It's just what he *wouldn't!*" she could still
impress upon me. "I was sure, at any rate," she added,
"that he didn't. But he denied certain occasions."

"What occasions?"

"When they had been about together quite as if Quint
were his tutor—and a very grand one—and Miss Jessel

only for the little lady. When he had gone off with the fellow, I mean, and spent hours with him."

"He then prevaricated about it—he said he hadn't?" Her assent was clear enough to cause me to add in a moment: "I see. He lied."

"Oh!" Mrs. Grose mumbled. This was a suggestion that it didn't matter; which indeed she backed up by a further remark. "You see, after all, Miss Jessel didn't mind. She didn't forbid him."

I considered. "Did he put that to you as a justification?" At this she dropped again. "No, he never spoke of it."

"Never mentioned her in connection with Quint?"

She saw, visibly flushing, where I was coming out. "Well, he didn't show anything. He denied," she repeated; "he denied."

This is pretty vague, but it does happen that children can try to seem more important to two lovers, let alone husband and wife, than the other person. And they will seem in competition with the older person. This has happened, because we all of us want to be liked more than someone else is liked. A child can get a triumph from thinking there is a secret between him and the boyfriend of his sister. This is comparatively minor, but it can take on bigger territory.

James is implying here that Miles felt he could mix up the arrangement between Quint and Jessel in such a way that Quint would find something more interesting in Miles than in her.

A good deal is implied, and this story in many ways is like *Hamlet*. There are so many things left out in *Hamlet*, so many questions possible. So with this. There are lots of things left out, but the things left out do serve the general purpose, which is the presentation of evil as an existent thing, but also shadowy, umbrageous, illusive, hardly graspable. It is a definite thing but hard to get at, like a name we've forgot; we know that it's there, but we just don't know where it is; and the more we fumble, the surer we are that there *is* something we are fumbling for.

We are at Section 10. One of the things Flora has learned is how to accuse others. The governess gets up in the night and finds Flora's little bed is empty, and the governess thinks she is out with Miss Jessel. Then Flora stands there "in so much of her candour and so little of her nightgown, with her pink bare feet and the golden glow of her curls." Before the governess can ask what she has been up to, Flora turns the tables and asks *her*. This is Flora:

> "You naughty: where *have* you been?"—instead of challenging her own irregularity I found myself arraigned and explaining. She herself explained, for that matter, with the loveliest, eagerest simplicity.

The governess presents herself as hardly perfect. She is not a master of repartee and doesn't come to *just* the right thing, she's no Bulldog Drummond, no Ronald Colman. She's a woman of some expedience but not all expedience, and she is delightfully human because she's at times at a loss.

There is a conversation, and Flora is presented as very astute.

> "Well, you know, I thought someone was"—she never blanched as she smiled out that at me.
> Oh, how I looked at her now! "And did you see anyone?"
> "Ah, *no!*" she returned, almost with the full privilege of childish inconsequence, resentfully, though with a long sweetness in her little drawl of the negative.

At that moment, in the state of my nerves, I absolutely believed she lied; and if I once more closed my eyes it was before the dazzle of the three or four possible ways in which I might take this up.

She isn't just hellbent on saying the child is a liar; she describes her own hesitations as she feels it must be so. To pursue the comparison again, the worst scene perhaps in *Hamlet* is when Hamlet is accusing his mother, and his mother says, "This is no way to act to a mother," and Hamlet is nonplussed—in fact, loses his aplomb; his deep boulevard manner is lost and he becomes a little bit of a truckdriver. He loses his finesse. Which happens. He cannot accuse his mother gracefully. The governess is in the same jam; she feels something is going on that's wrong, but how can she attack what is so close to her? She doesn't "take up" Flora's reply too definitely, and the section is again confused and this-and-that.

> Instead of succumbing I sprang again to my feet, looked at her bed, and took a helpless middle way. "Why did you pull the curtain over the place to make me think you were still there?"
> Flora luminously considered; after which, with her little divine smile: "Because I don't like to frighten you!"

All this going on with an air of gurgling and patter—it is very taking.

In the next passage, it seems that Quint, because the governess has stood up to him so well, is now afraid of her. She says the following:

> But I never met him there again; and I may as well say at once that I on no other occasion saw him in the house. I just missed, on the staircase, on the other hand, a different adventure. Looking down it from the top I once recognized the presence of a woman seated on one of the

lower steps with her back presented to me, her body half bowed and her head, in an attitude of woe, in her hands. I had been there but an instant, however, when she vanished without looking round at me. I knew, none the less, exactly what dreadful face she had to show; and I wondered whether, if instead of being above I had been below, I should have had, for going up, the same nerve I had lately shown Quint. Well, there continued to be plenty of chance for nerve.

This is well told. Now quite obviously, Miss Jessel isn't having the time of her after-life in coming here. If she is one of these fiends who just loves to torment mortals, I don't see it. She's there, pretty well whipped. "Her body half bowed and her head, in an attitude of woe, in her hands." What an unenterprising ghost! If the governess were simply in competition with Miss Jessel, I don't believe she would present her that way; she would present Miss Jessel as doing all kinds of wicked but profitable things. That is the way a woman who doesn't have much sense describes an enemy. She doesn't present her in this fashion.

Then seeing and not seeing goes on with Mrs. Grose:

But she was a magnificent monument to the blessing of a want of imagination, and if she could see in our little charges nothing but their beauty and amiability, their happiness and cleverness, she had no direct communication with the sources of my trouble.

The seeing of evil is never entirely pleasant. The governess shows misgivings. She has to see further than people like Mrs. Grose do, and it is not comfortable. When we are compelled to see something as bad which has looked good, it is not one of the pleasantest occasions—if we are sincere. And sometimes we have to.

The governess acts as if she knew there was something going on in the world which is bad. Now, James was exactly like that. James felt there was something awful going on among people—he didn't know exactly what it was—and he couldn't stand it. It hurt him to see it, and occasionally he tried to think it wasn't so. He points it out in various works, and here all his works are one: there is something that goes on in people's minds and the way they are with other people, that is just abhorrent. He hints at it again and again, and he isn't wholly glad at seeing it. Occasionally he has to say it and he is very pained in saying it. He is like the governess.

James saw there was something bad and, in fact, I think that one of the reasons he didn't pursue his studies sociologically was that at a very early age he felt there was something false in the relations of people to people *in a room;* and he was so appalled by this that he didn't study the falsity of what went on in a Paris factory or a factory in a Paris suburb. He was taken by what he saw as the meaning, but also as the falsity, of people with people. And that discovery was enough to last him for the rest of his life. He was always elaborating on it.

We are at Section 12, and we have these paragraphs. The governess is talking to Mrs. Grose about the children:

> "Why, of the very things that have delighted, fascinated, and yet, at bottom, as I now so strangely see, mystified and troubled me. Their more than earthly beauty, their absolutely unnatural goodness. It's a game," I went on; "it's a policy and a fraud."
> "On the part of little darlings—?"
> "As yet mere lovely babies? Yes, mad as that seems!" The very act of bringing it out really helped me to trace

it—follow it all up and piece it all together. "They haven't been good—they've only been absent. It has been easy to live with them, because they're simply leading a life of their own. They're not mine—they're not ours. They're his and they're hers!"

This passage has to do with some of the eternal problems, the abiding ethical questions and the subtleties of ethics. Mrs. Grose says:

"Quint's and that woman's?"
"Quint's and that woman's. They want to get to them."
Oh, how, at this, poor Mrs. Grose appeared to study them! "But for what?"
"For the love of all the evil that, in those dreadful days, the pair put into them. And to ply them with that evil still, to keep up the work of demons, is what brings the others back."

The question arises, what were the demons doing, that was so bad? Now I think if anyone said to a person: "You've heard of demoniacal possession?"—"Oh, sure, sure."—"Do you think it's good?"—"No, of course not; demoniacal, that's bad."—"Why is it bad?"—"Let me see."

The thing to be remembered is that the devil is someone who gives you a quick means of having your way when you don't have it in this world. He's Quick-way Mephistopheles. He's the person who says, "Well, if this world ain't so good to you, why can't you try another one? It's easy, we could work it." And then because he gives you something, he takes you over. And so you give up your soul.

What James is saying is this: "Something is going on in these children that is *very* extraordinary. Now, all you Londoners and all you Americans and all you French,

you don't see that; however, if I can get in a few supernatural things, maybe you'll believe it more." He felt
that for this purpose, the supernatural should get in,
and he was successful.

Well, in this section, Section 12, the uncle is described.
There has been some talk of perhaps informing the uncle
of what has been going on.

> Mrs. Grose considered, following the children again.
> "Yes, he do hate worry. That was the great reason—"
> "Why those fiends took him in so long? No doubt,
> though his indifference must have been awful. As I'm
> not a fiend, at any rate, I shouldn't take him in."

This uncle is presented as one who wants to take his
ease, away. He wants to be untroubled. Such uncles have
been elsewhere. This uncle is desirous *unusually* of ease.
The governess is disappointed in him. It could be said,
as will be noted later, she is disappointed because he
doesn't care for her too much. In the passage I have just
read, the governess gets quite emphatic. The uncle is
seen by her as uncaring, and he is also seen as having
been deceived: deceived by persons who are described
by the governess rather strongly as "fiends"—that is,
Quint and Jessel.

Though there are really no obvious goings on between
the governess and the uncle, the governess does seem
to have a sense of her own honor. This is a mighty thing;
it is very much in James, but it has been in all writing
of any depth: the way a person sees himself, the things
that he can do and cannot do. A good deal of drama
has to do with honor.

We have an example of that in what the governess
says at the end of this section. She may be fumbling in

some ways, but there is one thing that she wouldn't
take; if Mrs. Grose asks for help from the uncle, the
governess says, she will leave the place and Mrs. Grose
and everything. This is the passage:

> My companion, after an instant and for all answer, sat
> down again and grasped my arm. "Make him at any rate
> come to you."
>
> I stared. "To *me?*" I had a sudden fear of what she
> might do. " 'Him'?"
>
> "He ought to *be* here—he ought to help."
>
> I quickly rose, and I think I must have shown her a
> queerer face than ever yet. "You see me asking him for a
> visit?" No, with her eyes on my face she evidently
> couldn't. Instead of it even—as a woman reads another—
> she could see what I myself saw: his derision, his amuse-
> ment, his contempt for the breakdown of my resignation
> at being left alone and for the fine machinery I had set in
> motion to attract his attention to my slighted charms. She
> didn't know—no one knew—how proud I had been to
> serve him and to stick to our terms; yet she none the less
> took the measure, I think, of the warning I now gave her.
> "If you should so lose your head as to appeal to him for
> me—"
>
> She was really frightened. "Yes, Miss?"
>
> "I would leave, on the spot, both him and you."

This is pretty intense; it is as intense as anything in
this story. The governess sees her relation to this as
something that shouldn't be meddled with for the wrong
reason. If the uncle really wanted to find out about the
children, I'm sure the governess wouldn't mind that;
but having him come and try to smooth things over and
not try to understand what was going on—is just too
much. The governess doesn't want to give the appearance either of trying to have him interested in her for
a false reason. She is here like Jane Eyre, and *Jane Eyre*
is a book in which honor is present very much.

3

The Patter of Satan's Feet

In Section 13, feelings grow lower; things have a routine appearance. There is a combination of routine and terror that we have seen earlier. In this section we have a notation on how the children find out about the governess' life and how she has a hard time finding out about their lives:

> It was in any case over *my* life, *my* past, and *my* friends alone that we could take anything like our ease—a state of affairs that led them sometimes without the least impertinence to break out into sociable reminders.

We occasionally get phrases like "my friends." Who the governess' friends are, James doesn't say at all. It is teasing: you could think at other times the governess had no friends whatsoever. These are little side matters that James just leaves: they are laundry tickets without a person.

And the weather is changing. James, like any sensible person, is very much interested in the weather. If you're not interested in the weather, philosophically you are not exploiting all of life's opportunities. The weather is a very rich matter; it is something besides rainy, fair, moderate, and so on.

The summer had turned, the summer had gone; the autumn had dropped upon Bly and had blown out half our lights. The place, with its grey sky and withered garlands, its bared spaces and scattered dead leaves, was like a theatre after the performance — all strewn with crumpled playbills.

That is an interesting simile. You could have it another way. You could say that after the performance of Weton's Revenge, after the audience had left, the theatre was strewn with discarded playbills, as if they were leaves left by a late October wind. Or you could do— which is more unusual—what James has done: you could say that the place, "with its bared spaces and scattered dead leaves, was like a theatre after the performance—all strewn with crumpled playbills."

This is the beauty of a simile: you can start either way. James is not using the customary order; he is comparing a natural thing to an artificial thing, an earlier thing to a later one. Usually, it's the other way. You could say that the disorganized army scattered like leaves. If you said the leaves scattered like a disorganized army—that's a little unusual, though it could be said. James's simile gets in the theatre, and here one could have a little excursus on James's feelings about the theatre, but this excursus will not be.

So autumn is coming. And that is one thing, it seems, ghosts haven't interfered with: the coming of autumn. One doesn't know the seasons that ghosts prefer—it seems they come at any season. A very good month, I've heard, is April, when the weather changes from one thing to another. October is also very nice. I think Wilkie Collins preferred his ghosts to roam in October for that reason: there is a change from one kind of weather to another.

We have in this section a statement about the "lovely upward look" of the boy:

> —the lovely upward look with which, from the battlements above me, the hideous apparition of Quint had played.

This lovely upward look is something to remember. We have it in some Renaissance paintings: children look very deep and sweet. Some of Raphael's children are very meditative; they even have their finger on their chin, and they look up: "What shall I do next, God, for you?" Cherubims. Miles has this lovely upward look. It has been used by children very much. Every child knows that if he is accused by the teacher of anything, the first thing he should do is to look up and look sweet. However, if he wants to have the teacher pity him, he should look down. Either way is useful. However, if he's a delinquent, he stares at the teacher. But the lovely upward look, as if how could this be of *you?* is very useful indeed, and children get to the technique of it. It can be used quite effectively. Anyway, Miles seems to have it. I expect it of him.

In the next section, there are passages showing Miles thought pretty well of himself and was quite regardful of himself. This passage shows Miles thought he was somebody:

> Turned out for Sunday by his uncle's tailor, who had had a free hand and a notion of pretty waistcoats and of his grand little air, Miles' whole title to independence, the rights of his sex and situation, were so stamped upon him that if he had suddenly struck for freedom I should have had nothing to say.

This shows that the governess is rather conservative. Miles has a sense of what's coming to him. If we think something is coming to us that isn't, we can call it vanity; if we think that something is coming to us that is, we can call it dignity, honor, pride. The implication is that Miles thinks things are coming to him that are of vanity, arrogance, and a belief that one belongs to the fortunate classes.

We have Miles pleased with himself. He is showing confidence and he thinks he has quite delicately awed the governess.

> *NOTE. On the way to church, Miles upsets the governess by suddenly telling her he wants to go back to school, and suggesting his uncle be informed of this. Since the subject of his expulsion from the previous school has never been mentioned between them, the governess is considerably taken aback by this—so much so, that she lets Miles, Flora, and Mrs. Grose precede her into the church while she remains outside in the churchyard.—Ed.*

The business was practically settled from the moment I never followed him. It was a pitiful surrender to agitation, but my being aware of this had somehow no power to restore me. I only sat there on my tomb and read into what my little friend had said to me the fulness of its meaning; by the time I had grasped the whole of which I had also embraced, for absence, the pretext that I was ashamed to offer my pupils and the rest of the congregation such an example of delay. What I said to myself above all was that Miles had got something out of me and that the proof of it, for him, would be just this awkward collapse. He had got out of me that there was something I was much afraid of and that he should probably be able to make use of my fear to gain, for his own purpose, more freedom. My fear was of having to deal with the intolerable question of the grounds of his dismissal from school, for that was really but the question of the horrors gathered behind.

The last sentence is worth noting. There is the constant relation in James between the earthly bad thing and the bad thing that goes deeper. Miles has been dismissed from school; the governess feels that there is a relation between the ordinary event of Miles's being dismissed from school and the other thing, with the ghosts, which is much deeper and somewhat goes beyond this earth. She uses the phrase, "the question of the horrors gathered behind"; this should be seen in relation to the whole sentence, where we have the school matter related to the other, stranger matter.

This has been one thing in technique: if you want somebody to believe in an angel, have the angel rightly placed as to an ordinary farmer. If you want somebody to believe in the supernatural, have—if the supernatural presents evil—that supernatural related to an evil which is not supernatural. The two will help each other. Earth is the signpost to hell and heaven.

That his uncle should arrive to treat with me of these things was a solution that, strictly speaking, I ought now to have desired to bring on; but I could so little face the ugliness and the pain of it that I simply procrastinated and lived from hand to mouth.

She seems to think, as other ladies do, that the uncle would see her superficially. She doesn't want that. She wants to interest him, and she has the confusion that other ladies have in the James novels. They have two great desires: they want to interest a man, and then there is a desire which is a little greater—they want to interest him for a good reason. And this causes trouble in any decade.

> The boy, to my deep discomposure, was immensely in the right, was in a position to say to me: "Either you clear up with my guardian the mystery of this interruption of my studies, or you cease to expect me to lead with you a life that's so unnatural for a boy."

The natural life for an English boy of high degree was to be in a school. The governess knows something is going on which the uncle would not understand, and that is the deep reason for her hesitation. It is the feeling Hamlet would have if he had to explain to Polonius what's going on in him. That's not for him.

> What was so unnatural for the particular boy I was concerned with was the sudden revelation of a consciousness and a plan.
> That was what really overcame me, what prevented my going in. I walked round the church, hesitating, hovering; I reflected that I had already, with him, hurt myself beyond repair.

What is implied here is this: Miles feels that the governess knows too much. He feels he can fool anybody. Children think that; they feel that already adults are dead pigeons. Miles has been able to put things over on Mrs. Grose, his uncle, perhaps others; but the governess goes deeper, she just wants to know too much. One way he sees he can foil the governess is to have the uncle come through *her* asking, and then there will be one of those things corresponding to a "committee investigation": that is, investigation by a certain party of doings by the same party. Miles feels that if the uncle comes, the uncle will be in an angry mood: "I told you I didn't want to be disturbed, and what's this nonsense going on around here? I guess Miles is a little too much for you, huh?" And out of that the governess would be humiliated, she would feel she hadn't been seen right, and maybe she would leave, and things could go on merrily.

Why is the governess hurt, and just what is her feeling about Miles, and why does she feel Miles is trying to get her into a situation she wouldn't like? It isn't entirely clear, but I believe that if you look at all this closely, there will be something like what I've just said.

Miles, in a natural way, without showing his hand, wants the governess to make some complaint to the uncle so that, when the complaint is looked into, there'll be a saying, "You're too nervous, you make too much of what really doesn't go on at all. How can such things be?" The governess says:

> Therefore I could patch up nothing, and it was too extreme an effort to squeeze beside him into the pew; he would be so much more sure than ever to pass his arm into mine and make me sit there for an hour in close, silent contact with his commentary on our talk.

What seems to have been gone after by Miles is this: if he can get her in church and sit with her, and they can appear very friendly, in the house of God, then it would seem to those there that the governess was approving of him, and he was exculpated, he was nice. And the governess doesn't want that to happen.

Since I am now dealing with the story very intensively, I'd like to point out that all literature in the long run consists of words, and how they are placed. One of the most important things to desire is that one read in terms of the final and also the basic element in literature, which is the word. Out of that comes, in prose, the sentence; and in poetry, the line. The two are related, but in both poetry and prose there is the word and how the word is placed as to other words.

The word is the substance, from one point of view; and the placing as to other words is form. Both poetry and prose have that, and the sentence and the line can be seen as basic instances. Therefore, the word is important in any story of depth and worth; and the sentence is important, and the placing of words. A person who is careful is careful about how he chooses the word and places it.

James is careful in this story. He is careful usually, but in *The Turn of the Screw*, both conscious care and a deeper, unseen care are present.

We have come to the section where the governess and Mrs. Grose discuss the not having gone to church by the governess. The children didn't want Mrs. Grose to talk about it. Miles has been discreet. Mrs. Grose says to the governess:

> "No; Master Miles only said, 'We must do nothing but what she likes'!"
> "I wish indeed he would! And what did Flora say?"
> "Miss Flora was too sweet. She said, 'Oh, of course, of course!'—and I said the same."
> I thought a moment. "You were too sweet too—I can hear you all. But none the less, between Miles and me, it's now all out."

There are certain phrases that show what an author is getting at. One of the phrases in what was just read is, "You were too sweet too." Now, James like everybody else wanted to be sweet, but authentically sweet. Sweetness here is used in its deepest sense: the sign of non-corruption. When a thing is sweet, a fruit, it is not corrupted yet; chemically it hasn't altered for the satanic or the worse. But there is another kind of sweetness which is the simulation of that; and by now, when a girl is said to be "sweet," it is usually taken as a word of disparagement—because the imitation has been around so much, the imitation has come to be the customary thing. However, the word itself is still in good standing. And the governess doesn't want that which has afflicted all social life, and has to until people know themselves better: the imitation of sweetness. Without that imitation, civilization could hardly go on; but without it, too, civilization could get on better.

The business of in and out is also important in James. Those of you who are somewhat learned in his works will have noticed that he is fond of *in* and *out* and *it*. These have great meaning: three little monosyllables, two of them beginning with *i*. But with James, a person who is not able to be "out" is one whom really the gods do not favor. There is something so wonderful in the ability to be "out." In contradistinction, the disability is to be looked on with reproach and also with regret. Occasionally a person is "out," and sometimes it's a thing that is "out."

> "But none the less, between Miles and me, it's now all out."
> "All out?" My companion stared. "But what, Miss?"
> "Everything. It doesn't matter. I've made up my mind."

In James there is a good deal of feeling that two people can be together for a long time and they're not really "out"; in fact, the whole novel can be about the hope of being "out." James was aware of the fact that proximity does not mean communication. That is one of the morals that we get from James's works: proximity does not mean communication. And James, to make a pun of it of a sort, would say that proximity is really approximity, if that.

When the governess came back to the house from church, she saw the ghost of Miss Jessel in the school-room; this, combined with the fact that Miles and Flora act so smoothly as if nothing had happened, make her and Mrs. Grose, as they talk things over, decide that the uncle, after all, has to be written to. Interest now is to be centered strongly on this letter.

We are at Section 17:

I went so far, in the evening, as to make a beginning. The weather had changed back, a great wind was abroad, and beneath the lamp, in my room, with Flora at peace beside me, I sat for a long time before a blank sheet of paper and listened to the lash of the rain and the batter of the gusts. Finally I went out, taking a candle; I crossed the passage and listened a minute at Miles's door. What, under my endless obsession, I had been impelled to listen for was betrayal of his not being at rest, and I presently caught one, but not in the form I had expected. His voice tinkled out. "I say, you there—come in." It was a gaiety in the gloom!

I went in with my light and found him, in bed, very wide awake, but very much at his ease. "Well, what are *you* up to?" he asked with a grace of sociability in which it occurred to me that Mrs. Grose, had she been present, might have looked in vain for proof that anything was "out."

I stood over him with my candle. "How did you know I was there?"

"Why, of course I heard you. Did you fancy you made no noise? You're like a troop of cavalry!" he beautifully laughed.

"Then you weren't asleep?"

"Not much! I lie awake and think."

I had put my candle, designedly, a short way off, and then, as he held out his friendly old hand to me, had sat down on the edge of his bed. "What is it," I asked, "that you think of?"

"What in the world, my dear, but *you*?"

"Ah, the pride I take in your appreciation doesn't insist on that! I had so far rather you slept."

"Well, I think also, you know, of this queer business of ours."

I marked the coolness of his firm little hand. "Of what queer business, Miles?"

"Why, the way you bring me up. And all the rest!"

I fairly held my breath a minute, and even from my glimmering taper there was light enough to show how he smiled up at me from his pillow. "What do you mean by all the rest?"

"Oh, you know, you know!"

I could say nothing for a minute, though I felt, as I held his hand and our eyes continued to meet, that my silence had all the air of admitting his charge and that nothing in the whole world of reality was perhaps at that moment so fabulous as our actual relation. "Certainly you shall go back to school," I said, "if it be that that troubles you. But not to the old place—we must find another, a better. How could I know it did trouble you, this question, when you never told me so, never spoke of it at all?" His clear, listening face, framed in its smooth whiteness, made him for the minute as appealing as some wistful patient in a children's hospital; and I would have given, as the resemblance came to me, all I possessed on earth really to be the nurse or the sister of charity who might have helped to cure him. Well, even as it was, I perhaps might help! "Do you know you've never said a word to me about your school—I mean the old one; never mentioned it in any way?"

He seemed to wonder; he smiled with the same loveliness. But he clearly gained time; he waited, he called for guidance. "Haven't I?" It wasn't for *me* to help him— it was for the thing I had met!

Something in his tone and the expression of his face, as I got this from him, set my heart aching with such a pang as it had never yet known; so unutterably touching was it to see his little brain puzzled and his little resources taxed to play, under the spell laid on him, a part of innocence and consistency. "No, never—from the hour you came back. You've never mentioned to me one of your masters, one of your comrades, nor the least little thing that ever happened to you at school. Never, little Miles—no, never—have you given me an inkling of anything that *may* have happened there. Therefore you can fancy how much I'm in the dark. Until you came out, that way, this morning, you had, since the first hour I saw you, scarce even made a reference to anything in your previous life. You seemed so perfectly to accept the present." It was extraordinary how my absolute conviction of his secret precocity (or whatever I might call the poison of an influence that I dared but half to phrase) made him, in spite of the faint breath of his inward trouble, appear as accessible as an older person—imposed him almost as an intellectual equal. "I thought you wanted to go on as you are."

It struck me that at this he just faintly coloured. He gave, at any rate, like a convalescent slightly fatigued, a languid shake of his head. "I don't—I don't. I want to get away."

"You're tired of Bly?"

"Oh, no, I like Bly."

"Well, then—"

"Oh, *you* know what a boy wants!"

I felt that I didn't know so well as Miles, and I took temporary refuge. "You want to go to your uncle?"

Again, at this, with his sweet ironic face, he made a movement on the pillow. "Ah, you can't get off with that!"

I was silent a little, and it was I, now, I think, who changed colour. "My dear, I don't want to get off!"

"You can't, even if you do. You can't, you can't!"—he lay beautifully staring. "My uncle must come down, and you must completely settle things."

"If we do," I returned with some spirit, "you may be sure it will be to take you quite away."

"Well, don't you understand that that's exactly what I'm working for? You'll have to tell him—about the way you've let it all drop: you'll have to tell him a tremendous lot!"

The exultation with which he uttered this helped me somehow, for the instant, to meet him rather more. "And how much will *you*, Miles, have to tell him? There are things he'll ask you!"

He turned it over. "Very likely. But what things?"

"The things you've never told me. To make up his mind what to do with you. He can't send you back—"

"Oh, I don't want to go back!" he broke in. "I want a new field."

He said it with admirable serenity, with positive unim- peachable gaiety; and doubtless it was that very note that most evoked for me the poignancy, the unnatural childish tragedy, of his probable reappearance at the end of three months with all this bravado and still more dis- honour. It overwhelmed me now that I should never be able to bear that, and it made me let myself go. I threw myself upon him and in the tenderness of my pity I em- braced him. "Dear little Miles, dear little Miles—!"

My face was close to his, and he let me kiss him, simply taking it with indulgent good-humour. "Well, old lady?"

"Is there nothing—nothing at all that you want to tell me?"

He turned off a little, facing round toward the wall and holding up his hand to look at as one has seen sick chil- dren look. "I've told you—I told you this morning."

Oh, I was sorry for him! "That you just want me not to worry you?"

He looked round at me now, as if in recognition of my understanding him; then ever so gently, "To let me alone," he replied.

There was even a singular little dignity in it, some- thing that made me release him, yet, when I had slowly risen, linger beside him. God knows I never wished to harass him, but I felt that merely, at this, to turn my back on him was to abandon or, to put it more truly, to lose him. "I've just begun a letter to your uncle," I said.

"Well, then, finish it!"

I waited a minute. "What happened before?"

He gazed up at me again. "Before what?"

"Before you came back. And before you went away."

For some time he was silent, but he continued to meet my eyes. "What happened?"

It made me, the sound of the words, in which it seemed to me that I caught for the very first time a small faint quaver of consenting consciousness—it made me drop on my knees beside the bed and seize once more the chance of possessing him. "Dear little Miles, dear little Miles, if you *knew* how I want to help you! It's only that, it's nothing but that, and I'd rather die than give you a pain or do you a wrong—I'd rather die than hurt a hair of you. Dear little Miles"—oh, I brought it out now even if I *should* go too far—"I just want you to help me to save you!" But I knew in a moment after this that I had gone too far. The answer to my appeal was instantaneous, but it came in the form of an extraordinary blast and chill, a gust of frozen air and a shake of the room as great as if, in the wild wind, the casement had crashed in. The boy gave a loud, high shriek, which, lost in the rest of the shock of sound, might have seemed, indistinctly, though I was so close to him, a note either of jubilation or of terror. I jumped to my feet again and was conscious of darkness. So for a moment we remained, while I stared about me and saw that the drawn curtains were unstirred and the window tight. "Why, the candle's out!" I then cried.

"It was I who blew it, dear!" said Miles.

This is a complex section and it has to be seen in some multiple fashion.

The governess is confused about Miles. She feels that Miles has taken to evil, and she wants to be sympathetic. She is aware that if she is too sympathetic, she'll be taken advantage of, as she is here. As soon as she makes an approach that is taken to be forgiveness, that is too warm, Miles gets sarcastic, derisive, blows out the candle, and so on.

The governess, it must be said, is awkward; she fumbles. She cannot put together sympathy with Miles and her anger at what he's up to. She isn't too clear, that must be admitted; and so when she gets somewhat too gooey with him, Miles is repelled. But Hamlet also fumbles.

We have, at the beginning of this section, a scene of the sort that is in many novels of the 19th century: people trying to write letters. Sometimes there is a great gust of wind outside, sometimes there isn't. But people have to write important letters, and they sit by the window, and they have a time. It can be said, with just pessimism, that one reason for not being born is, you may have to write letters you don't want to write. If you're never born, you won't have that difficulty.

So the governess goes to listen at Miles's door. She thinks that if Miles is having all this trouble, why doesn't he show it a little? Why shouldn't he be agitated like Coleridge was in his sleep, or like all people who have done misdeeds? If you've done a crime, how dare you not show it? But Miles doesn't oblige.

> His voice tinkled out. "I say, you there—come in." It was a gaiety in the gloom!

This is typical; it shows the savoir faire that Miles has.

> . . . it occurred to me that Mrs. Grose, had she been present, might have looked in vain for proof that anything was "out."

The governess does fumble; she cannot believe things are bad. This occasionally occurs: because of the sweetness of the social procedure, you don't think there is something terrible going on. The governess has had this disagreement with Miles, but everything now is so cordial, you'd think there had been no such difficulty.

> I stood over him with my candle. "How did you know I was there?"
> "Why, of course I heard you. Did you fancy you made no noise? You're like a troop of cavalry!" he beautifully laughed.

A governess who was trying to conceal wouldn't have put down this jest.

> "What is it," I asked, "that you think of?"

And then, such an evasion. Husbands have used it. "What are you thinking of so much?"—"Dear, of you, of course."

> "What in the world, my dear, but *you?*"
> "Ah, the pride I take in your appreciation doesn't insist on that! I had so far rather you slept."
> "Well, I think also, you know, of this queer business of ours."

There is a kind of known ambiguity, because "this queer business" has to do with the strange business of the ghosts and then the more ordinary business of the school; and both find it convenient to go to the school.

> I marked the coolness of his firm little hand. "Of what queer business, Miles?"
> "Why, the way you bring me up. And all the rest!"

People here are firmly vague.

"What do you mean by all the rest?"
"Oh, you know, you know!"

This has various motifs. There is the motif of candor, the motif of innocence, the motif of wickedness about school difficulty, and then there is the other; and they are mingled.

The governess can't make up her mind about Miles. There is something that takes her in him. She is falling for the same thing that Quint and Miss Jessel fell for: Miles can show so deftly that he likes you. Almost anybody would fall. He is very clever at that. When we have this cultivated boy, perhaps coming from an old Norman family, who knows?—smiling at us and jesting with us, and here we are, the daughter of a clergyman —to have him look at us in that deep way—flesh and blood, particularly flesh and blood of not the upper classes, would, I think, be very much affected. Quint and Jessel were, and the governess has some of the weakness of them.

His clear, listening face, framed in its smooth whiteness, made him for the minute as appealing as some wistful patient in a children's hospital.

The fact that he can show himself weak to her is taken by her as a great compliment. This comparison of a wistful patient in a children's hospital, I don't believe is one that hints at all kinds of subterranean carnalities. If any lady really were going after some of the more Cyprian sins, I don't believe she would describe the object as a wistful patient in a children's hospital.

In a subtle way, the governess has been flattered. She knows it's absurd for Miles to say he's been thinking only about her, but she does fall for it somewhat.

He seemed to wonder; he smiled with the same loveliness. But he clearly gained time; he waited, he called for guidance.

The two moods of the governess are here shown: "the same loveliness" and "but he clearly gained time." A woman is like that: on the one hand, she just wants to be useful, everything is sweet, come to my arms, I'll dry your tears; and on the other: what's all this about? The moods are changing. Miles is really rather surprised that the governess is so knowing and makes so much trouble; he's looking her over. She isn't so strong; in fact, he thinks she has done quite a few weak things, but still she is too smart for a person in her position. The governess goes off the track too. The matter of the ghosts interests her more really than the school matter; but she can talk about the school more conveniently.

"Therefore, you can fancy how much I'm in the dark. Until you came out, that way, this morning, you had, since the first hour I saw you, scarce even made a reference to anything in your previous life. You seemed so perfectly to accept the present."

Miles was able to admit something about the school, and that has taken the governess, but, to be sure, the other matter is still not talked about. However, in this section we have a more definite intimation of Miles's later weakness. Flora seems to be more decided than he is. He can't change, but he cannot go on with the old way; and that is why, as we'll see, his heart stops beating. Miles is less tough than Flora is, in terms of the story, anyway.

To think that here he is being so brave and charming, and then he is taken by these evil things, that this evil machine is working in him—the governess then does go too far and she sympathizes with him too utterly, and she makes a false move. She says so.

> It overwhelmed me now that I should never be able to bear that, and it made me let myself go. I threw myself upon him and in the tenderness of my pity I embraced him.

She says pity. We can have our way by working on the pity of others.

> "Dear little Miles, dear little Miles—!"

I must say that at this moment, the governess is as weak as anywhere in the story. But she is not presented as wholly knowing her mind. If Hamlet could have such trouble making up his mind, if Othello could be a hero and still so weak, if Antigone in Sophocles could have her weakness, if Orestes could, if all the tragedies have strong people who are weak—then why can't the governess also be silly?

> My face was close to his, and he let me kiss him, simply taking it with indulgent good-humour. "Well, old lady?"

This indulgent good-humor is really a kind of scorn: "Well, you may be pretty strong, governess, but you sure are not strong all the time."

> "Is there nothing—nothing at all that you want to tell me?"

This phrase has often been used to make another person slightly contemptuous. Mothers have used it inopportunely.

Then we have:

> . . . it made me drop on my knees beside the bed and seize once more the chance of possessing him.

She uses the word "possessing" in somewhat of the sense other than ownership, but still it isn't good. She thinks she wants to help him. But there is this desire to help and to think that only you can help, which is in the idea of possession. Possession implies the idea of an infinite possibility of nursing. There are other things in it, but apparently that is what is most attractive to the governess.

> "Dear little Miles, dear little Miles, if you *knew* how I want to help you! It's only that, it's nothing but that, and I'd rather die than give you a pain or do you a wrong— I'd rather die than hurt a hair of you."

This doesn't seem to be the governess who was so keen and looked at Miss Jessel. It's the other governess —just as Hamlet, again, is sometimes very firm and other times not.

> "Dear little Miles"—oh, I brought it out now even if I *should* go too far—"I just want you to help me to save you!"

The saving takes on too much of a maternal air, and Miles doesn't like it, and the governess is mistaken— she's weak that much. Saving ought to be in another framework.

But I knew in a moment after this that I had gone too far. The answer to my appeal was instantaneous, but it came in the form of an extraordinary blast and chill, a gust of frozen air and a shake of the room as great as if, in the wild wind, the casement had crashed in.

James is pretty subtle; he's using these melodramatic effects but he still is subtle. On the one hand, the boy is very frightened: "This is not the way to see me." On the other, the governess, having been rather stupid, is seen as someone Miles has triumphed over; but the triumph makes him terrified.

The boy gave a loud, high shriek, which, lost in the rest of the shock of sound, might have seemed, indistinctly, though I was so close to him, a note either of jubilation or of terror.

James is aware that at certain times a thing that may terrify us is also a triumph for us. And the elements are at one with Miles here. You'd think that it was the gust of frozen air and the shake of the room that might have put out the candle, but he says *he* did it. There is a oneness of Miles with the turbulent elements.

I jumped to my feet again and was conscious of darkness. So for a moment we remained, while I stared about me and saw that the drawn curtains were unstirred and the window tight. "Why, the candle's out!" I then cried.
"It was I who blew it, dear!" said Miles.

This is a subtle section. There are two people. There is Miles with a certain arrangement of weakness and strength, and he is hoping that he can get strength in some new way; he also hopes that his older way has been correct. So he is going from weakness to strength or from strength to weakness, whichever way you want to look at it. The governess is too; she is really angry with Miles, she knows there is something very bad, but she also can be taken by the same thing that Quint was taken by: a certain kind of charm. So as she writes this letter, she hesitates and she goes parleying, and in the parleying she acts with some excess, and Miles doesn't like it. But the governess is not wholly lost, as we'll see. She doesn't wholly win; in tragedies, people don't wholly win. But things are not lost, something is won.

Miles, as a character, is distinctive because, whereas the co-presence of good and evil was shown to be in adults in literature of the past, here in a serious way this co-presence is shown to be in a child. The villainy is vague; it is not like the villainy in *Dr. Jekyll and Mr. Hyde.* I don't believe yet that in the penal code of England there is a crime called Getting Power Over Supernatural Visitors, or Dominating Spectres Who Go Jumping Over Fences. Miles is not committing the kind of villainy that Scotland Yard in its busyness would go after; and also he is a child. Yet the villainy is there, and it seems to be of a deeper sort because it is occurring so early in life.

The *child* being this way, the *child* being specious and sincere, gentle and scheming, deceptive and frank —that is a discovery. In a way it corresponds to the great disillusion that many Victorian ladies and gentlemen had to undergo for a while when pondering the significance of Darwin's discoveries. It was very cruel. Here was man, going to Oxford, and related to beings who jumped from branch to branch and uttered strange sounds. It was very disillusioning. I may say, people got over it; people do get over their shocks in history.

But the shock of seeing what a child is like, I believe, will be harder to get over.

And here it is well to say that a faint shock was felt by people who, say twenty years after *The Turn of the Screw*, pondered on the message of Dr. Freud. Dr. Freud did make children out to be unspeakable, horrible, unendurable, simian, polymorphous in their sexual desires; but they were made out so *crudely* horrible that people, when they saw them as horrible, felt it wasn't their children. Somehow they were reading Dr. Freud's mystery story; somehow they were reading something in the way of science fiction, even though it had footnotes. It couldn't be the child they had been giving a little stick of candy to: *he* wasn't polymorphous. It was all too weird.

And it happens now that the approach to children of James is affecting people more than Freud's is, because Freud hit the nail on the head too long. It was easy to be not disillusioned about Freud, because you never had any illusion of any big sort: it was just not the children you knew. But the presentation here of a child having the duality that man is thought to have—and does have —that is something else; and though this story hasn't been as sensational as the impact of Freud, I believe it is on the move.

In the next passage, it is the following day, and the governess is thinking of Miles and the meaning of what occurred:

Say that, by the dark prodigy I knew, the imagination of all evil *had* been opened up to him: all the justice within me ached for the proof that it could ever have flowered into an act.

This brings up another matter: how much do we have to do things that are evil before we can be called evil? There are some statements of a pretty thorough kind. In the New Testament, Christ says that he who hath committed adultery in his heart is already a sinner. Legally, however, you can think anything you please. I bring this up because it has to do with the question, where does evil exist and when does it become evil? Does evil need an act? The governess is very thoughtful about Miles and Flora; she thinks that maybe things are going on in Miles's mind, but he is really too beautiful to have all those bad things flower into an act.

The idea of something bad is very deep and common. One of the most curious things about the word *bad* is that it is something a child hears first, one of the earliest words; someone—a mother or an aunt—is ready to tell a child he is bad or good, and in the meantime, the world is still trying to find out what the word *bad* means. One question is, just where does bad begin, when do you begin being bad?

In ordinary historical terms, evil has not begun until it affects another; that is, until it shows itself. It is true that evil has been seen as within; but in a historical or political or legal sense, evil is something seen as having emerged: if it doesn't emerge, it is that much not evil. And though this cannot serve entirely, still one has to think of why the distinction has been made. The easiest thing to see is that if anybody is thinking evil thoughts, if you don't know about them, tra-la-la-la-la, who cares? You're not going to be hurt because somebody wants you to drop into a well. But still, if we knew that somebody wanted us to drop into a well, we wouldn't like it.

A deep reason for persons' making a distinction between thought and action—outside of the practical reason—is this: if evil comes forth, it means that when you saw it in you, you weren't enough against it. Many people, when they have evil thoughts, take them lightly, and in fact, they play around with them. They say: "This is very interesting, I'm such a nice person outside, but what I think of is something!" People really do juggle evil thoughts as people used to juggle coins in their pockets: in order to feel rather prosperous. This has to do with why the distinction has been made. If evil does come out, it means that while evil was present, you did not do enough to extinguish its power.

There is one thing then that must be said about evil: whether it is in its budding state, its middle state, its flagrant state, you have to be against it; and your not having been against it is implied when it happens. People therefore should not feel that having an evil thought is equivalent to evil at its fulness, but it is evil in terms of substance.

The presence of evil is useful because you have a chance to be against it. You cannot say it can't come, because it will; but the time of its coming is the time to be against it. However, since people know that others don't know their evil thoughts, they begin playing around with them, and to play around with them is a good way for them to become more effective. Because as soon as you give a half-welcome or a third of a welcome to something, it may change to a full welcome—outside of the fact that the pampering of evil, however faintly, is that which tends to disintegrate the whole being. One of these days there may be an exact description of what an evil thought does to the chemistry of the body, the organization of the body. It is my opinion right now that it doesn't do it much good.

The governess is in a state where she wants to be clearer; she says she aches for proof. If the "imagination of all evil" had "flowered into an act," then it means that evil in its "within" form had been welcomed: there was not sufficient opposition to it. There is some opposition all the time, but there is opposition to good too; so because there is really less opposition to evil than there is to good, evil can win out. It's not because there is no opposition at all. But the governess would either like to have proof that the thoughts she imagines are just thoughts, or that they have "flowered into an act," as the phrase is here. We can be in a state where we are not sure whether another person, a person close to us, is good or bad; this is not very pleasant, but it is very common.

NOTE. This meditation of the governess takes place the day after Miles blew out the candle. That afternoon, she says, Miles appears, and:

He had never, at any rate, been such a little gentleman as when, after our early dinner on this dreadful day, he came round to me and asked if I shouldn't like him, for half an hour, to play to me.

Miles is extremely sweet to the governess and beguiles her the whole afternoon, playing the piano enchantingly. She almost forgets the ghosts and the letter to the uncle. Suddenly, she realizes Flora is missing, and she suspects that Miles has intentionally distracted her so that Flora could go off with Miss Jessel.—Ed.

We have come to the part where Mrs. Grose and the governess have gone looking for Flora by this strange, meaningful lake. Mrs. Grose, as usual, wishing not to grant children their full abilities, has asked: "All alone —that child?" And the governess who is, as usual, severer, says: "She's not alone, and at such times she's not a child: she's an old, old woman."

The quality of this sentence, in its utterness, is hardly duplicated anywhere else in James, or for that matter, in any other work. Not that children haven't been seen as horrid. But this way of writing about a child, saying she is an old woman, is somewhat different. There is another dimension. The question arises then, why is James using that term?

The thing about "old" is that there is a tendency, with age, to contract, and as one contracts, to be more protected and also to be more selfish. So if James is considering his words carefully, he is trying to say that Flora had that quality of contraction.

Flora's favorite place, the governess says, is the lake, so she and Mrs. Grose go looking for her there. They find she has taken the boat and rowed across. They walk around to the other side and find the boat. The governess says:

> It had been intentionally left as much as possible out of sight and was tied to one of the stakes of a fence that came, just there, down to the brink and that had been an assistance to disembarking. I recognized as I looked at the pair of short, thick oars, quite safely drawn up, the prodigious character of the feat for a little girl.

Here we can see the great desire of the little girl. As they say in Indian language: Much energy, much purpose. Or to make it a little more unrefined: Heap big purpose, heap big energy. This little girl has a definite purpose, so she is very strong. She is an "old woman," but strong as anything.

> There was a gate in the fence, through which we passed, and that brought us, after a trifling interval, more into the open.

This sometimes happens: things have been in the underbrush, and then you reach space.

Then, "There she is!" we both exclaimed at once.

This is the Jamesian war cry: "There she is!" or "There it is!" I imagine when James is translated into French, there are many *voilàs*.

Flora, a short way off, stood before us on the grass, and smiled as if her performance was now complete.

That is a quite complacent sentence.

The next thing she did, however, was to stoop straight down and pluck—quite as if it were all she was there for —a big, ugly spray of withered fern.

That is quite obviously symbolic, because it brings together the child idea and the old woman idea. She is stooping to conquer, but also to acquire ugliness.

She waited for us, not herself taking a step, and I was conscious of the rare solemnity with which we presently approached her.

So Flora and Mrs. Grose and the governess have met, and there is a moment of great solemnity.

She smiled and smiled, and we met; but it was all done in a silence by this time flagrantly ominous.

James is careful. It could have been put this way: "We met and she smiled and smiled." But James wants the smile first and the "met" second, which is right. And "flagrantly ominous" is one of those examples of an adverb being shattering and dynamic while the adjective is quiet.

In the meantime, since I think that James was aware of *Hamlet* as he wrote this, we have a verbal reminiscence of some importance in the "she smiled and smiled." It is put in such a way that the *Hamlet* rhythm is insisted on. The exact phrase is in Act I, Scene 5. Hamlet says:

> Meet it is I set it down,
> That one may smile, and smile, and be a villain.

And Flora smiled and smiled.

Mrs. Grose, even though she sees the child smiling, acts like the surrogate mother. She wants to break the spell:

> Mrs. Grose was the first to break the spell: she threw herself on her knees and, drawing the child to her breast, clasped in a long embrace the little tender, yielding body.

Here is a question of appearance and reality: a little tender body that smiles as Claudius does.

> While this dumb convulsion lasted I could only watch it, which I did the more intently when I saw Flora's face peep at me over our companion's shoulder.

The feeling is that Flora is complacent: "You see, I've still got a friend. Nobody believes you. Everybody is for me." Children can be that way. "No matter what bad things you do, people will vote for you." It is true, too.

> "The flicker had left it; but it strengthened the pang with which I at that moment envied Mrs. Grose the simplicity of *her* relation.

The governess, being uncertain, says: I wish I could take children at their face value the way Mrs. Grose, at least part of the time, can. How relieving it would be! And it would be relieving. If we could go just by how people seem, it would be really quite refreshing.

We have, then, the governess showing that even as she is doing all of this, there is something in her that regrets it. Then we have a charming sentence:

> Still, all this while, nothing more passed between us save that Flora had let her foolish fern again drop to the ground.

She doesn't need the fern now.

> What she and I had virtually said to each other was that pretexts were useless now.

That is another point. Pretexts were useless with Miles, and now they are useless with Flora. There is going to be something like a slam-bang battle.

> When Mrs. Grose finally got up she kept the child's hand, so that the two were still before me; and the singular reticence of our communion was even more marked in the frank look she launched me. "I'll be hanged," it said, "if *I'll* speak!"

Mrs. Grose is two ways. She can agree with the governess while she is talking to the governess, but as soon as she sees the adorable child, that bit of irresistibleness, that love where all journeys end, she forgets the logic she has shown a little with the governess, and she comes into a team for a while with Flora. This means that people are not steady.

Then Flora, being somewhat reassured by Mrs. Grose, does a bit of crowing:

> It was Flora who, gazing all over me in candid wonder, was the first. She was struck with our bareheaded aspect. "Why, where are your things?"
> "Where yours are, my dear!" I promptly returned.

And Flora is saying: "Look, ladies, this is really too careless; I'd better get you in hand. This is too much: ladies shouldn't go without their hats." Wise little Flora. But things were going on with all of them too important for them to think of hats. This is in the governess' answer.

> She had already got back her gaiety, and appeared to take this as an answer quite sufficient.

She doesn't want to carry this on too openly.

> "And where's Miles?" she went on.
> There was something in the small valour of it that quite finished me.

These children are very composed. In every situation they show savoir faire. They remind one of the well-bred English officer who meets a jaguar—it's all in serving the Empire.

> These three words from her were, in a flash like the glitter of a drawn blade, the jostle of the cup that my hand, for weeks and weeks, had held high and full to the brim and that now, even before speaking, I felt overflow in a deluge.

The implication again is that Flora knew mighty well that Miles, in another part of the forest, to put it that way, is going through the same business that she is. They cover the estate pretty well. But Flora acts as if she never heard of such things. The governess does get somewhat perturbed. She says:

> "I'll tell you if you'll tell *me*—" I heard myself say, then heard the tremor in which it broke.

Courageous governess!

> "Well, what?"
> Mrs. Grose's suspense blazed at me.

Mrs. Grose is now recovering herself after that hug.

> But it was too late now, and I brought the thing out handsomely."

Courageous lady!

> "Where, my pet, is Miss Jessel?"

We have this gallant language: Where, my dear, is the ammunition? This is, then, smooth and frightening, and it seems so sunny and gentle.

The showdown between Flora and the governess comes in the next section. So, going on with the text:

> Just as in the churchyard with Miles, the whole thing was upon us.

In other words, the showdown began in the churchyard with Miles, when Miles wanted her to go inside the church and seem to be for him. Now there is going to be a showdown with Flora: "I know what you're doing, and you admit it!" The governess' mentioning Miss Jessel's name stands for this.

Much as I had made of the fact that this name had never once, between us, been sounded, the quick, smitten glare with which the child's face now received it fairly likened my breach of the silence to the smash of a pane of glass. It added to the interposing cry, as if to stay the blow, that Mrs. Grose, at the same instant, uttered over my violence—the shriek of a creature scared, or rather wounded, which, in turn, within a few seconds was completed by a gasp of my own. I seized my colleague's arm. "She's there, she's there!"

Miss Jessel stood before us on the opposite bank exactly as she had stood the other time, and I remember, strangely, as the first feeling produced in me, my thrill of joy at having brought on a proof.

For the moment she acts as if she is grateful to Miss Jessel: "The fact that you now make an appearance, just when I want you to!"

She was there, and I was justified; she was there, and I was neither cruel nor mad. She was there for poor scared Mrs. Grose, but she was there most for Flora; and no moment of my monstrous time was perhaps so extraordinary as that in which I consciously threw out to her— with the sense that, pale and ravenous demon as she was, she would catch and understand it—an inarticulate message of gratitude.

If the governess is so much against Miss Jessel, why should there be any message of gratitude? This means that the governess doesn't know everything: at least, she doesn't act completely symmetrically. She is contradictory.

The next sentence is quite horrid. Miss Jessel is always arising erect:

She rose erect on the spot my friend and I had lately quitted, and there was not, in all the long reach of her desire, an inch of her evil that fell short.

Miss Jessel could be angry because she was made to appear when she didn't want to. She was evoked at the wrong time, but she is sending evil out, and "not an inch of her evil fell short."

> This first vividness of vision and emotion were things of a few seconds, during which Mrs. Grose's dazed blink across to where I pointed struck me as a sovereign sign that she too at last saw, just as it carried my own eyes precipitately to the child.

The governess here feels that Mrs. Grose saw dimly that something was going on. She saw more than she ever had, but she recoiled. She could not continue the seeing. Mrs. Grose in this sentence has a "dazed blink," and she is, the governess thinks, maybe seeing what she saw.

> The revelation then of the manner in which Flora was affected startled me, in truth, far more than it would have done to find her also merely agitated, for direct dismay was of course not what I had expected.

What Flora does is to become hard and still: rigid. She stiffens more. One gathers that Miles bends more than Flora does.

> Prepared and on her guard as our pursuit had actually made her, she would repress every betrayal; and I was therefore shaken, on the spot, by my first glimpse of the particular one for which I had not allowed.

Flora becomes stony and retaliatory. The governess has always "not allowed" for something.

> To see her, without a convulsion of her small pink face, not even feign to glance in the direction of the prodigy

I announced, but only, instead of that, turn at *me* an expression of hard, still gravity, an expression absolutely new and unprecedented and that appeared to read and accuse and judge me—this was a stroke that somehow converted the little girl herself into the very presence that could make me quail.

This can be called a massive impudence, and it does frighten the governess.

This is one of the crucial chapters, and the tone in which it is written has to do with what the story is about. The fact is that the governess is not accredited. She points out Miss Jessel, and Mrs. Grose says she doesn't see anything. This would be disabling to her credibility if it were not a constant motif in James's works. Frequently people are seeing something that is going on and are trying to tell somebody else, and the other people see nothing. They see the front and the poor visionary sees the back. So he or she is not believed. A good deal in James is about how people are trying to convey something and they have very hard work of it, and sometimes there is no conveyance at all.

If, then, because she is not accredited here, it means that the governess has not seen anything, this would not be in keeping with the whole tenor of James's works: that every now and then a person sees something and he cannot convey it to others, and they in turn have a hard time believing this was seen.

We do know that ghosts are seen selectively. In Shakespeare there is a great discord. Banquo can see the witches and Macbeth can see the witches, but when Banquo comes to the banquet, only Macbeth can see Banquo, all the others don't. When Hamlet's father visits the conversation of Hamlet and his mother, the mother does not see Hamlet's father. That makes for difficulties.

The conversation, in fact, is almost broken up because of that. Ghosts are selective. You can see one kind of ghost at one time and not at another time. Various people can see ghosts, and you don't know who is going to have the right to see them. It seems that Mrs. Grose doesn't have the right. Either she doesn't have the right, or the governess doesn't see them either. It happens frequently that something is seen by one person and not by another. The way this section is written, we see the governess saying that what she had seen was not accredited, but she is not too angry with Mrs. Grose for saying, "Oh, no, I see nothing, Miss"—though it is one of the disillusioning things. "Look at this!" she says, and Mrs. Grose sees nothing.

But the governess, being a good governess, tells all, even what is against her; and that is why she is a real James character. James characters are always telling of their defeats. You can't be a James character unless you luxuriate in your defeats.

The other thing is this: in *What Maisie Knew,* when Maisie tries to tell her mother something of the meaning of what she saw, the mother gets very angry and calls her names. But this doesn't mean at all that Maisie hadn't seen something. It simply means that the mother didn't like what she saw. Other people in the novel didn't see what Maisie saw. Maisie sees more, and therefore gets into more trouble. Maisie is like the governess. If the governess is to be discredited because there are not other witnesses to bear her out, then other characters, including Maisie, would also be discredited.

The governess doesn't see everything. I think she doesn't see Miss Jessel completely. I think Miss Jessel is also a little angry with Flora. The governess thinks

Miss Jessel and Flora are working together completely: there I disagree. But the governess essentially sees.

Going on with the text. Mrs. Grose at this point consists of a "flushed face" and a "loud, shocked protest, a burst of high disapproval." Then she says something:

> "What a dreadful turn, to be sure, Miss! Where on earth do you see anything?"

Mrs. Grose is ready to give the governess up by this time. The governess says:

> "You don't see her exactly as *we* see?—you mean to say you don't now—*now?*"

The governess is intense. One of the interesting things here is that the "we" seems to include the governess and Flora, which means that the governess has a sense of kinship with Flora, and that means in turn that the governess feels she could give in to some of the things that Flora does.

There are italics around here pretty often, and the governess is still intense:

> "Only look, dearest woman, *look*—!" She looked, even as I did, and gave me, with her deep groan of negation, repulsion, compassion—the mixture with her pity of her relief at her exemption—a sense, touching to me even then, that she would have backed me up if she could.

This sentence is like a very sad ripple, the last ripple of an evening. Mrs. Grose would like to help the governess, but she just doesn't see anything at all, and can't do anything for her. She just is unmoved; she cannot see things the way the governess can, so help her God. The sentence has the fall of a statement meaning, "I've done all I could, and I'm sorry but I can't do anything more."

But soon Mrs. Grose changes again, and starts to reassure Flora:

"She isn't there, little lady, and nobody's there—and you never see nothing, my sweet!"

In fact, I'm afraid Mrs. Grose at this moment is getting patronizing. It is bad enough to call Flora "little lady," but "little lady" and "my sweet" are too much. Mrs. Grose gets back to her old way of seeing. She goes on:

"How can poor Miss Jessel—when poor Miss Jessel's dead and buried?"

That's the most sensible thing in the whole book! Then she tries to win over the governess, and says—still to Flora—very patronizingly:

"*We* know, don't we, love?" —and she appealed, blundering in, to the child. "It's all a mere mistake and a worry and a joke—and we'll go home as fast as we can!"

Our companion, on this, had responded with a strange, quick primness of propriety, and they were again, with Mrs. Grose on her feet, united, as it were, in pained opposition to me.

Flora continued to fix me with her small mask of reprobation, and even at that minute I prayed God to forgive me for seeming to see that, as she stood there holding tight to our friend's dress, her incomparable childish beauty had suddenly failed, had quite vanished.

So the governess thinks she is too harsh. It is interesting to see Flora holding Mrs. Grose's dress.

I've said it already—she was literally, she was hideously, hard; she had turned common and almost ugly.

Then the little girl opens up:

"I don't know what you mean."

And this is said a little like a piston rod:

"I see nobody. I see nothing. I never *have*. I think you're cruel. I don't like you!"
Then, after this deliverance, which might have been that of a vulgarly pert little girl in the street, she hugged Mrs. Grose more closely and buried in her skirts the dreadful little face.

It is very vivid. Flora is playing politics now. Then she does that which children can do: she produces "an almost furious wail." I imagine James heard some of these, and like all adults in a state of confusion and distress, didn't like it.

In this position she produced an almost furious wail. "Take me away, take me away—oh, take me away from *her!*"

And the governess is still surprised:

"From *me?*" I panted.

I imagine the governess shouldn't be so surprised by now.

"From you—from you!" she cried.

Mrs. Grose is somewhat embarrassed. The governess says:

For Mrs. Grose I had an imperative, an almost frantic "Go, go!" before which, in infinite distress, but mutely possessed of the little girl and clearly convinced, in spite of her blindness, that something awful had occurred and some collapse engulfed us, she retreated, by the way we had come, as fast as she could move.

Then the governess is so sick of the whole matter (sick in the ethical sense) that she is just tired and wants to get away from it. She wants to get away from trying to change little girls and making them good; she wants to get away from trying to convey ideas to Mrs. Grose; she wants to get away from winning over Miss Jessel. She has a period, which many heroines have, of sobbing in grief, "Oh, why was it thus!" Most often it is done on a bed. Usually there is some pounding of the pillow. Then after a while you get tired, and then your mother calls for you when it gets to be supper-time. Here it occurs on the ground:

> I must have lain there long and cried and sobbed, for when I raised my head the day was almost done.

There is very often intense prayer in the forest; then sometimes the morning comes. Here the night comes:

> I got up and looked a moment, through the twilight, at the grey pool and its blank, haunted edge, and then I took, back to the house, my dreary and difficult course.

That is a sentence which is very grey and thuddy and quite beautifully constructed. It has the beauty of Gray's *Elegy:*

> The Curfew tolls the knell of parting day,
>   The lowing herds wind slowly o'er the lea,
> The plowman homeward plods his weary way,
>   And leaves the world to darkness and to me.

Now fades the glimmering landscape on the sight,
   And all the air a solemn stillness holds . . .

There is a certain fall of syllables, and there is a similarity to the James sentence.

Then the mood freshens:

When I reached the gate in the fence, the boat, to my surprise, was gone, so that I had a fresh recollection to make on Flora's extraordinary command of the situation.

The governess is looking about. She is standing up, and she sees that she has a contender who is very smart.

4

Chatter About Depravity

WE ARE in Section 20. It is a while after the governess has come back from the lake alone, and she says:

> On the removal of the tea-things I had blown out the candles and drawn my chair closer; I was conscious of a mortal coldness and felt as if I should never again be warm.

Things are cozy, and they are cozy in coldness. You feel that the governess is cozy in herself, thinking; but there is an emptiness and a coldness. That is a situation that many people can get into: something seems very intimate, but the intimacy itself is cold. This sentence is one of the most aromatic.

Next we have Miles:

> So, when he appeared, I was sitting in the glow with my thoughts. He paused a moment by the door as if to look at me; then—as if to share them—came to the other side of the hearth and sank into a chair.

It seems for a moment as if the power of evil has taken in both the governess and Miles, and they are both admitting it. It is just a very big thing, and hard to beat: a little bit like the old devil sea or the Mississippi River—it breaks all the dykes.

We sat there in absolute stillness; yet he wanted, I felt, to be with me.

That is a nice touch. Miles, in his way, tries to show compassion for the governess.

We come to Section 21, and the governess once more, as people will, gets encouraged and thinks something should be done. She can't resign. She thinks that after Miles has visited her and showed a quiet desire to be in communication, maybe she can talk to Miles. She sees Flora as even worse than Miles. He, at least, hasn't opened up in that terrifying way: the way she calls "vulgar" and "pert."

I may say at this point, as to the eradication of evil, that one cannot say the story ends as if evil had lost, because it hasn't. But we do get the idea that evil can be seen; at least you can talk about it. It is there, and the governess is correct in seeing it. The story does say, "Continued in our next, and maybe under better circumstances evil can be defeated."

Before a new day, in my room, had fully broken, my eyes opened to Mrs. Grose, who had come to my bedside with worse news.

Flora is in a state of turbulence about the governess, so it seems.

It was not against the possible re-entrance of Miss Jessel on the scene that she protested—it was conspicuously and passionately against mine.

We haven't lived if someone hasn't said of us, "Take him away," or "Take her away." The best people have that happen to them: "I can't stand the sight of you." So the governess, being a person, has that happen to her. Flora says, "I can't stand her, take her away."

Occasionally one gets the feeling that James wanted to point out Flora and Miles as being of the ruling class of England and therefore of a higher breed than the governess. We have something of that here. The governess, being the daughter of a clergyman not the daughter of a squire with a landed estate, was looked down upon by Flora, who was more favorably circumstanced from an hereditary point of view.

The governess says:

> "She'll never speak to me again."
> Hideous and obscure as it all was, it held Mrs. Grose briefly silent; then she granted my point with a frankness which I made sure had more behind it. "I think indeed, Miss, she never will. She do have a grand manner about it!"

In this little speech, Mrs. Grose shows that she also thinks Flora doesn't regard the housekeeper and the governess as ladies. She says, "She do have a grand manner about it!" That is ungrammatical, but it happens to be an English idiom, like "I says" in America.

> "And that manner"—I summed it up—"is practically what's the matter with her now!"

That is interesting, because it is put on a class basis. The governess describes Flora's manner as a thing wrong with her, "practically what's the matter with her now!" So there is a tie-up between the domination of Miss Jessel by Flora and the domination that the governess hints at in this speech. In other words, an interest-

ing bit of investigation would be: Why does the governess say this? Is there any tie-up between what the
governess says of Flora's manner and the attitude of
Flora to people? I think there is.

The governess still thinks she can do something with
Miles, and she wants Mrs. Grose to take Flora to the
uncle in London. Mrs. Grose says:

> "Your idea's the right one. I myself, Miss—"
> "Well?"
> "I can't stay."

Here James is showing his sense of climax and mon-
tage. Mrs. Grose has heard these things from Flora which
have given her ideas about what is really going on. Now
James brings this out with intensity.

> The look she gave me with it made me jump at possibili-
> ties. "You mean that, since yesterday, you *have* seen—?"
> She shook her head with dignity. "I've *heard*—!"
> "Heard?"
> "From that child—horrors! There!" she sighed with
> tragic relief. "On my honour, Miss, she says things—!"
> But at this evocation she broke down; she dropped with
> a sudden sob, upon my sofa and, as I had seen her do be-
> fore, gave way to all the grief of it.

Mrs. Grose is affected! The picture she had of Flora
she can have no more.

> It was quite in another manner that I, for my part, let
> myself go. "Oh, thank God!"

And though Mrs. Grose has been disillusioned and has
come to see evil where she didn't want to see it—that is,
in Flora—it is all quite satisfactory for the governess,
because she has been vindicated.

She sprang up again at this, drying her eyes with a groan.

Mrs. Grose doesn't understand that "thank God." Why should you thank God because evil has been seen in a child? But you can thank God if you think evil is in a child, and you are worried about whether it really is; and then at least you see you haven't been a sensationalist, haven't gone around imputing awfulness to people who don't have awfulness. So the governess says:

> "It so justifies me!"
> "It does that, Miss!"
> I couldn't have desired more emphasis, but I just hesitated. "She's so horrible?"
> I saw my colleague scarce knew how to put it. "Really shocking."
> "And about me?"
> "About you, Miss—since you must have it. It's beyond everything, for a young lady; and I can't think wherever she must have picked up—"

So Flora has been showing what she felt about the governess, and it is quite shocking.

> "The appalling language she applied to me? I can, then!" I broke in with a laugh that was doubtless significant enough.

The little phrase, "I can, then!" is worth looking into.

As I have said, the things that children can think about their mothers, say under their breath about their mothers, sometimes say to their mothers—are pretty strong, pretty awful. The words that little innocents of three-and-a-half or five-and-a-half have used about or to their mothers, would really look like some of the bolder sections of Joyce. It is not just the obscenity: it is the feeling that is present. I should say that one half-hour out of every twenty-four is spent in unmitigated cursing, as things go. Mothers are appalled sometimes by hearing some of the language a youthful denizen of Park Avenue might use. The child lets his mother have it.

The phrase of the governess, "I can, then!" is the most important thing here. The implication is that Flora and Miles have learned from the two visitors, Quint and Jessel, how to despise people. Obscenity and shocking phrases are examples of language as contempt. This kind of language is a way of scorn, a way of haughtily-deflating ego. The implication is that the children have been learning this from the visitors.

Going on, Mrs. Grose says:

> "But I must go back."
> I kept her, however. "Ah, if you can't bear it—!"
> "How can I stop with her, you mean? Why, just *for* that; to get her away. Far from this," she pursued, "far from *them*—"
> "She may be different? she may be free?" I seized her almost with joy. "Then, in spite of yesterday, you *believe*—"

The governess is not talking in one way here. However, she shows her good design by saying of Flora, "She may be different? she may be free?" About believing, Mrs. Grose answers:

> "In such doings?" Her simple description of them required, in the light of her expression, to be carried no further, and she gave me the whole thing as she had never done. "I believe."

That is one of the high points of the story. It is true there is no evidence that Mrs. Grose has actually seen the visitors. But there is something she feels about the

way Flora talks. It is not given. Perhaps James felt he
couldn't give just what it was that Flora said. There is
a phrase in "Christabel":

> A sight to dream of, not to tell!

How was it that Flora talked, and how was it that this
talk of hers affected Mrs. Grose so much, and through
it she came to see that the governess was right? The
implication is that only through something beyond earth
as we customarily see it, could Flora be this way.

The question here is: what made Mrs. Grose say in
this solemn manner, "I believe." James doesn't say. But
even with the paucity of detail, there is a feeling of
credibility. The governess says:

> Yes, it was a joy, and we were still shoulder to shoulder:
> if I might continue sure of that I should care but little
> what else happened.

The reason for that is in keeping with other works of
James: there is a witness, somebody who will back you
up. This is needed. The characters in James want someone to say, "What you see makes sense."

The governess is so glad she isn't making up things,
that her perceptions are just:

> My support in the presence of disaster would be the same
> as it had been in my early need of confidence, and if my
> friend would answer for my honesty, I would answer for
> all the rest.

She needs somebody to think she is telling the truth.

Now Mrs. Grose tells the governess something about
the letter she sent to the uncle:

"Your letter won't have got there. Your letter never went."

"What then became of it?"

"Goodness knows! Master Miles—"

"Do you mean *he* took it?" I gasped.

She hung fire, but she overcame her reluctance. "I mean that I saw yesterday, when I came back with Miss Flora, that it wasn't where you had put it. Later in the evening I had the chance to question Luke, and he declared that he had neither noticed nor touched it."

Earlier we had the appearance of someone called "the maid"; now we have someone called Luke. He isn't much around anywhere else, as far as I can see, but it is good to know that he has a name and he exists. A name is more than the governess ever gets.

We could only exchange, on this, one of our deeper mutual soundings, and it was Mrs. Grose who first brought up the plumb with an almost elated "You see!"

That is getting into more complicated territory. It is a strange metaphor. There is a way of sounding the ocean. You send something down which is called a plumb, and the plumb will tell you how deep the water is. So Mrs. Grose and the governess have been sending down the plumb, "making deep mutual soundings," all for the purpose of finding out just what Miles did or didn't do. It does seem strange to have to go exploring the bottom of the sea to find out what Miles was doing, but that is the way it is. The justification is that Miles's mind is like the bottom of the sea.

"Yes, I see that if Miles took it instead he probably will have read it and destroyed it."

"And don't you see anything else?"

I faced her a moment with a sad smile. "It strikes me that by this time your eyes are open even wider than mine."

Mrs. Grose is what is called a good body. She believes in all the virtues and the seven deadly sins. She believes that a person who is good has the virtues, and a person who is bad has the sins. It is all very convenient. Only, as later generations have known from the works they have read, the sins and the virtues have a way of disguising themselves and getting into each other's way and mingling. Still, stealing has never been wholly praised. Even these days, stealing is not looked upon as an act making one worthy of distinction.

They proved to be so indeed, but she could still blush, almost to show it. "I make out now what he must have done at school." And she gave, in her simple sharpness, an almost droll disillusioned nod. "He stole!"

I think, however, Miles was up to more things. But something as definite as stealing will suit Mrs. Grose very well.

I turned it over—I tried to be more judicial. "Well— perhaps."
She looked as if she found me unexpectedly calm. "He stole *letters!*"

"He stole *letters*" is worth looking at. Why letters? The symbol is this. If you can read another person's mail and the other person doesn't know it, you've got something on him: you've got him (or her) in your power. And so daughters, when they find that their mothers have been surreptitiously reading their mail, get to a high pitch of daughterly frenzy. There have been ever so many disputes about it.

Of course, one could say that Miles would want the money which is sometimes enclosed in letters, but there is no implication of that. If you have information about a person, then you have something on him.

So Mrs. Grose is going to take Flora to London, and the governess is quite excited:

> "Leave us, leave us"—I was already, at the door, hurrying her off. "I'll get it out of him. He'll meet me—he'll confess. If he confesses, he's saved."

The governess here talks quite jauntily. She feels everything is going her way, and she gets confidence. Miles will make the sun come through; the clouds will be driven away, the thickening dark will be made transparent. A lot she knows. One of the worst things about optimism is that we underestimate the insistency of evil.

The governess wants to feel that (1) evil can be understood; and (2) that once understood, it can be given the celestial heave-ho. These are her desires. She wants to be sure that she is seeing things clearly, not deceiving herself. She thinks if she sees and understands the evil in Miles, then that much she can see what is going on in herself. What may be going on in her is a tendency likewise to look on people amiss, to be unjust to them, to use them in the wrong way. She is worried about that, and that is why she was so careful with the uncle.

> The dear woman kissed me on this, and I took her farewell. "I'll save you without him!" she cried as she went.

This means that Mrs. Grose has come to see that the
governess is pretty careful, that she doesn't make people
worse than they are, and she wasn't unjust to Flora.
This is all put in the phrase, "I'll save you without him!"
Mrs. Grose has reached her most enthusiastic point.

We come to Section 22. This is written in the James
style, which has been found occasionally difficult, occasionally insuperable, and occasionally maddening.
James has a way of dealing with something which out-
wardly looks unimportant and then, by giving it almost
a comic tremendousness, pointing to the fact that there
is more there than people want to see.

Mrs. Grose and Flora are off to London, and the governess says:

> Yet it was when she had got off—and I missed her on
> the spot—that the great pinch really came.

When the governess consents to Flora's going to
London, she feels she won't be able to succeed with
Flora: the thing that might have been, wasn't. So the
governess is disappointed among other things.

> Now I *was,* I said to myself, face to face with the ele-
> ments, and for much of the rest of the day, while I fought
> my weakness, I could consider that I had been supremely
> rash.

The rashness seems to be that she had given up her
advantage in being a teacher. She had consented to
Flora's leaving, and Miles would look on her differently.
Also Miles might think she had given up about Flora,
and might take advantage of it. She has a tendency
to regret. The governess is one of those persons who
is regretting all the time. She is very human there.

In the previous section we came across someone called Luke. Here we suddenly find out that the place is replete with help; in fact, it is a beehive. One didn't think so before:

> What had happened naturally caused them all to stare; there was too little of the explained, throw out whatever we might, in the suddenness of my colleague's act.

That is Mrs. Grose.

> The maids and the men looked blank.

What could this be? Little girl goes from estate to London!

> . . . and I dare say that, to bear up at all, I became, that morning, very grand and very dry.

This means that no matter what all these maids and men may be gossiping about, she is going to act as if she never heard it. She is going to act like an aristocrat with the rabble whispering about. She is going to be "very grand and very dry." That must have been something. It would make a good scene, but I don't think any actress would be capable of it—somebody acting "very grand and very dry" because little girl goes off to London from estate. Various ladies might take this part, but I can think only of a combination of perhaps Rachel and Duse, if that.

> I welcomed the consciousness that I was charged with much to do, and I caused it to be known as well that, left thus to myself, I was quite remarkably firm.

That is a funny sentence. The governess sends little messages, "I am quite remarkably firm, whatever you

say." I don't know how she conveyed this. I don't know
what it is she was charged to do. If there is any aberra-
tion in the governess, I think it comes out here. All I
can see is that she doesn't have to teach anybody.

This is about Miles. She says:

> If so much had sprung to the surface, I scarce put it too
> strongly in saying that what had perhaps sprung highest
> was the absurdity of our prolonging the fiction that I had
> anything more to teach him.

Ordinarily this wouldn't be true, because a governess
usually knows some things that a boy somewhat over
ten hasn't learned yet. But the idea is to show that
Miles had a wisdom that was very unusual indeed.

> It sufficiently stuck out that, by tacit little tricks in which
> even more than myself he carried out the care for my
> dignity, I had had to appeal to him to let me off straining
> to meet him on the ground of his true capacity.

This means that the governess does not have to act
as if Miles were the ordinary learning child, and is a
repetition of the previous sentence. I think there is a
double meaning of "capacity." Capacity would take in
his ability to learn as such, but also an ability to see and
to be cunning which was more than the governess
could cope with, or be expected to cope with.

We come to an important statement:

> Here at present I felt afresh—for I had felt it again and
> again—how my equilibrium depended on the success of
> my rigid will, the will to shut my eyes as tight as possible
> to the truth that what I had to deal with was, revolt-
> ingly, against nature.

This sentence can be looked on in various ways. The phrase "against nature" has to be seen. Evil has to be considered as apart from the supernatural visitation. There are two things: one is the fact that there are these visitors; the other is, just what do they mean? There are ghost stories in which people appear, and there is not the feeling that they represent something repulsive. Very often ghosts are good. We don't feel, for example, that Banquo's ghost in *Macbeth* is revolting. He is simply a very important messenger.

We have the question of why this is called "against nature"? The implication is this. If nature were followed into its very depths, it would seem to be against nature. That is, the extreme of a certain way would seem so different from what we see ordinarily, that we might want to say it was supernature, or supernatural; or infra-nature, below the natural. This is expressed in the next sentence:

> I could only get on at all by taking "nature" into my confidence and my account, by treating my monstrous ordeal as a push in a direction unusual, of course, and unpleasant, but demanding, after all, for a fair front, only another turn of the screw of ordinary human virtue.

Since this brings us again to the title of the story, it has to be looked at.

What James is saying is this: I don't think I could make you believe just how far nature could go into evil unless I represented it to you as supernatural. When something in human beings is carried to the utmost and is seen, it would shock people so much, they would think they were in that which is beyond nature.

The ghosts are not the "turn of the screw." There is some way of mind which, because perception and action have gone deeper than usual, you can see clearly. The screw gets tighter the more you turn it. It gets tight at what can be called vanity pure. Vanity pure, once it were seen, would seem horrible, because vanity pure, as Aesthetic Realism sees it, comes to this. There wouldn't be a thing in this world outside of yourself that you wouldn't despise. There wouldn't be a thing which you wouldn't get pleasure from because you could make it look loathsome. In fact, you would see the whole universe as existing in order to be despised and give you glory.

When one sees the import of that, it does sound terrible. But it can be compared to Hamlet's accusation of himself because he had made the world look very unappetizing and dull. That is not as terrible as the thing James hints at—and besides, Hamlet puts it so well. But the tendency to fly-blow the whole universe so that your ego can win; the tendency to take every beautiful thing and to see it only as serving you, is the fulness of certain tendencies which, in ordinary civilization, are kept within bounds because people wouldn't stand for it if they weren't. If this fulness were seen, people would think it was in another world.

James did feel, though he couldn't say so, that the desire on the part of children to despise was a horrible thing. It is a horrible thing. Children can get the air with which people say, "Bring me a couple of musicians, let them play Chopin, pay 'em off and give 'em a bite"—this feeling that because you have more money than the musicians, you can order them around, you can buy up anything. Ego has been that way and can be that way; and, in fact, is going on that way now. Power makes you think you control everything.

So James was annoyed, and sometimes he was awkwardly annoyed. Let's say he was visiting a home where there was one of those intolerable velveteen brats, some scion of an old family. The first impulse of a child, particularly one spoiled by a mother, is to have contempt. All guests are seen with contempt by children whose mothers let them cultivate their ego and not-seeingness. James, as I see it, was very angry when he had one of these snotty juveniles of an old family take him for granted and not see him.

And he saw these early things as a sign. He felt: Can't we see the stinkweed in the bud, do we have to wait until it grows up? James saw the whole noxious flower. He had vision. The thing is, he could not express his vision in ordinary terms; that was not for him. He could not say, for example, to the mothers of England and America: "If these children don't have more of a sense of other people, and if the mothers and fathers don't teach their children to see snottiness as something not so good, I don't know what England will get to, or America." That he couldn't say, but he was indignant about it, and he put his indignation in the form of these two children. He put it symbolically, because he was of his time; but the symbol still stands.

We are now in Section 23. Miles and the governess have had dinner, and they are alone. The governess is going to broach things. Miles is standing by the window, looking out, and she says:

> But an extraordinary impression dropped on me from the boy's embarrassed back—none other than the impression that I was not barred now.

James is given to studying people's backs. He finds all kinds of messages in backs, and people have said it is because he injured his own back or something. Be that as it may, James is very much interested in finding knowledge in backs.

Here, the meaning is extracted from the boy's "embarrassed back." Well, it is a rich Jamesian sentence, so let us rejoice. "None other than the impression that I was not barred now"—and that is good. The boy is embarrassed. She extracts a meaning from it; and as she extracts a meaning, she has an extraordinary impression, and what is it? She isn't barred now! That is wonderful—such a way to knowledge!

> This inference grew in a few minutes to sharp intensity and seemed bound up with the direct perception that it was positively *he* who was.

And here knowledge goes on frighteningly, wonderfully. The impression has changed to an inference, which is good. The impression which was dropped on her now is an inference, which grows in a few minutes to "sharp intensity." But the inference is "bound up with the direct perception that it was positively *he* who was." So the inference that she wasn't barred gets to sharp intensity, and then gets bound with the inference that it was positively Miles who was barred.

Then surprisingly the governess says:

> He was admirable, but not comfortable: I took it in with a throb of hope.

I don't know if it is worth it to be admirable but not comfortable, but many people think it is. And she is now taking things in. That means things are developing. And there is "a throb of hope."

Wasn't he looking, through the haunted pane, for some-thing he couldn't see?—and wasn't it the first time in the whole business that he had known such a lapse?

The idea is, he is looking for Quint; but why is it that Miles can't find him? The implication is that Miles no longer wants to find him, but also that he is not com-fortable because he can't.

Miles, trying to act composed, says Bly agrees with him. Then he says to the governess:

> "Nothing could be more charming than the way you take it, for of course if we're alone together now it's you that are alone most. But I hope," he threw in, "you don't par-ticularly mind!"
>
> "Having to do with you?" I asked. "My dear child, how can I help minding?"

There is something in Miles that the governess wants to change and also wants to use to understand something in herself. So if there is not full communication, the governess does not mind. She goes on:

> "Though I've renounced all claims to your company—you're so beyond me—I at least greatly enjoy it. What else should I stay on for?"
>
> He looked at me more directly, and the expression of his face, graver now, struck me as the most beautiful I had ever found in it.
>
> "You stay on just for *that?*"

The governess has always wanted to see Miles as having a beautiful face, but also the face seems to show an interest in something of what the governess herself has to go for.

> "Certainly. I stay on as your friend and from the tre-mendous interest I take in you till something can be done

for you that may be more worth your while. That needn't surprise you."

The language here is somewhat evasive, and the phrase particularly so is "till something can be done for you that may be more worth your while."

My voice trembled so that I felt it impossible to suppress the shake.

This is because the governess has reached something of rock-bottom nature in herself. There can be a great experience. Other characters in James, when they come to grips, do tremble, because when people really talk about themselves, there is something of a trembling nature. When self meets self, ordinary life has been put aside, so why shouldn't there be trembling?

"Don't you remember how I told you, when I came and sat on your bed the night of the storm, that there was nothing in the world I wouldn't do for you?"

This sounds more ordinary, but what I think is being got at is this. If the governess does something for Miles, she would do it for herself; and therefore, since there is nothing in the world she wouldn't do for herself, there is nothing in the world she wouldn't do for Miles.

"Yes, yes!" He, on his side, more and more visibly nervous, had a tone to master; but he was so much more successful than I that, laughing out through his gravity, he could pretend we were pleasantly jesting.

She is much shaken by this kind of conversation. He is affected, too, but he can make more of a success of maintaining his savoir faire. He says:

"Only that, I think, was to get me to do something for *you!*"

Miles thinks the governess has a purpose, which she undoubtedly has. The purpose was, first of all, to find out what Miles was up to. If she understood that, she could take care of herself. So the accented *you* is to be looked at.

"It was partly to get you to do something," I conceded. "But, you know, you didn't do it."

Which is so.

"Oh, yes," he said with the brightest superficial eagerness, "you wanted me to tell you something."
"That's it. Out, straight out. What you have on your mind, you know."

The deepest things are said here, in this casual way.

"Ah, then, is *that* what you've stayed over for?"
He spoke with a gaiety through which I could still catch the finest little quiver of resentful passion;

And that must be something to put over—a gaiety through which one can catch "the finest little quiver of resentful passion." Aren't emotions wonderful?

but I can't begin to express the effect upon me of an implication of surrender even so faint.

And so we have gaiety, quiver of resentful passion, but there is also a melting, a yielding, an "implication of surrender"—faint, but it is there. So the richness of emotions is being seen.

It was as if what I had yearned for had come at last only to astonish me. "Well, yes—I may as well make a clean breast of it. It was precisely for that."

The governess says, Yes, I wanted to know what was on your mind, you know.

He waited so long that I supposed it for the purpose of repudiating the assumption on which my action had been founded; but what he finally said was: "Do you mean now—here?"

James's language gets complicated and difficult. The sentence could be put in the following way more simply: "He waited so long it seemed he was doing it for the purpose of showing I was wrong in what I had said." Assumptions go on being repudiated until we don't know what is going to happen; but a "repudiated assumption" is just something doubted.

"There couldn't be a better place or time." He looked round him uneasily, and I had the rare—oh, the queer!— impression of the very first symptom I had seen in him of the approach of immediate fear.

As Miles has to talk, or thinks even of talking about himself, there is fear. I have noticed that ever so many times. The greatest fear is to talk about something, and it is also the greatest hope. Miles, as we'll see, doesn't wholly talk about himself, and it is a pity. The spiritual obstetrics are not complete. The moral of all this is that people don't know what is good for them: such a tragic moral. Also people don't know what is good for other people, that is also true. It is a wonder the world goes on.

It was as if he were suddenly afraid of me—which struck me indeed as perhaps the best thing to make him. Yet in the very pang of the effort I felt it vain to try sternness, and I heard myself the next instant so gentle as to be almost grotesque. "You want so to go out again?"

So the governess wants Miles to fear her, but she can't go after that entirely. She has a hard time being stern; then she sees herself being so gentle as to be almost grotesque. What a time!

"Awfully!" He smiled at me heroically, and the touching little bravery of it was enhanced by his actually flushing with pain.

He likewise wants to talk now, but we are not going to have a happy birth.

He had picked up his hat, which he had brought in, and stood twirling it in a way that gave me, even as I was just nearly reaching port, a perverse horror of what I was doing.

When a boy, or anybody, picks up a hat and starts twirling it, it does come from a kind of nervousness; and there may be some complacency in it. The interesting word here is "perverse." The governess has pretty clearly presented the fact that having Miles talk would be a very good thing. If there is difficulty in her mind, it may come because she is not wholly for it herself. She has doubts herself, and this being so, she feels that she is asking a person to give up these dear things, and she is not the person to ask this. That is another thing from saying that Miles should not talk.

The governess cannot wholly say what she is after. I don't think James could wholly say. To affect a person very, very much is an act of violence, and it also can be the most beautiful thing going.

> To do it in *any* way was an act of violence, for what did it consist of but the obtrusion of the idea of grossness and guilt on a small helpless creature who had been for me a revelation of the possibilities of beautiful intercourse? Wasn't it base to create for a being so exquisite a mere alien awkwardness?

The governess at this moment becomes very unsure of herself. I'll say in advance that if the governess had not been so unsure of herself, Miles would have had an easier time, and Flora would have had an easier time too. The fact is that James felt he was unsure of himself as to certain things. Towards the end of his life, he was trying to get surer and surer. We must all try to get surer and surer. The governess is essentially right. If she were the person described by Edmund Wilson and some others, she would not tell her qualms here.

> So we circled about, with terrors and scruples, like fighters not daring to close. But it was for each other we feared!

That is true. The governess fears that if she has a person give up a kind of secret, that would mean she had no right to retain a secret for herself. You cannot really want another person to be frank, to use that word, unless you are ready to be frank yourself. Many people try. They ask other people to be honest while not sure of their own honesty.

If one wants to say that the governess was not honest enough to convince Miles, I think that can be said justly; but it is something else from saying the governess was on the wrong track.

Now Miles talks like a boy; he gets very emphatic, and
we feel he is getting into his childhood for a change:

> "I'll tell you everything," Miles said—"I mean I'll tell you
> anything you like. You'll stay on with me, and we shall
> both be all right and I *will* tell you—I *will*. But not now."

And we have the compromise of postponement.

> "Why not now?"
> My insistence turned him from me and kept him once
> more at his window in a silence during which, between
> us, you might have heard a pin drop.

It is surprising to see James use an old phrase, one of
the standbys of narrative, "you might have heard a pin
drop." Still, it is there; and it is a very effective phrase.
Many people would say it was a cliché. Maybe in the
1890's it wasn't so much of a cliché.

> Then he was before me again with the air of a person
> for whom, outside, someone who had frankly to be
> reckoned with was waiting. "I have to see Luke."

So we have Luke again. If one wants to be probing
and exact and a little unrelenting, as I do, Luke is what
can be called a surrogate for Quint. Luke would cor-
respond to the great population who aren't interested in
other people's feelings too much, and whom you can
have contempt for.

> I had not yet reduced him to quite so vulgar a lie, and
> I felt proportionately ashamed.

The governess feels that this kind of statement, his
having to see "Luke," is really too unhandsome.

But, horrible as it was, his lies made up my truth. I achieved thoughtfully a few loops of my knitting. "Well, then, go to Luke, and I'll wait for what you promise. Only, in return for that, satisfy, before you leave me, one very much smaller request."

The governess is piqued: "How long will this be postponed? He's going to Luke now." She seems to forgive him, but she really doesn't.

He looked as if he felt he had succeeded enough to be able still a little to bargain. "Very much smaller—?"
"Yes, a mere fraction of the whole."

What she brings up now would affect him very much, and it does. What happens is that because the governess shows pique in this fashion, and seems to want to use one thing to get at another, Miles comes back to his old way, and there is a big fight in him between the grandeur, as he sees it, of the old way, and what might be a new way. Still, we have to take this section as we have it. The governess goes on:

"Tell me"—oh, my work preoccupied me, and I was off-hand!—"if yesterday afternoon, from the table in the hall, you took, you know, my letter."

So we come to the last section of the James story. There are very few resounding, clear victories in this world, and at the time James wrote this story, there was more of a tendency to have a story end without the kind of climactic conclusion that had been seen as necessary before. *The Turn of the Screw* ends in a kind of fadeout, and therefore is to be seen as serving a purpose of James. What James saw was that something good always puts up a fight, and doesn't entirely lose; but usually it doesn't win in any external manner, because things have a way of going on. However, within the draw, one can see a certain drift.

There are some matters which a human being, in ordinary life, doesn't really decide. As Aesthetic Realism sees it, most people go to their graves with the big things undecided. Every tombstone could have on it: "I didn't decide the biggest things." There isn't enough vision and decision in ordinary life. The friction of one way on another is a wearing thing for a person. There are times when two emotions that always go on in us, come to a showdown, get into a frantic clasp; and then something even physiological can happen.

The reason Miles dies is because he can't decide. "Extinction through indecision" would be the aesthetic coroner's statement about him.

There is an example of a similar thing happening in a story by Hawthorne called "The Man of Adamant." This person is haughty, aloof, and he uses the Bible and communing with God for some of the damndest conceit and haughty segregation ever. The characters that we see elsewhere in Hawthorne are made compact and salient in this terrible creature: he is the Biblical snob turned to stone. He wants to be alone, to be in the contempt industry without interruption, to make it purer than ever. Hawthorne goes so far as to say that this person didn't want to go to heaven—because there would be angels to disturb him! That's how far Hawthorne goes.

But there is a girl, Mary Goffe, who tries to change Richard Digby. She tells him he has been wrong; he should not use the Bible to despise everything he can think of. He gets angry when she talks, and what happens to Miles happens to him. Yet it is quite clear that Mary Goffe was right. This is the passage:

"Tempt me no more, accursed woman," exclaimed he, still with his marble frown, "lest I smite thee down also! What has thou to do with my Bible?—what with my prayers?—what with my heaven?"

No sooner had he spoken these dreadful words, than Richard Digby's heart ceased to beat; while—so the legend says—the form of Mary Goffe melted into the last sunbeams, and returned from the sepulchral cave to heaven. For Mary Goffe had been buried in an English churchyard, months before; and either it was her ghost that haunted the wild forest, or else a dream-like spirit, typifying pure Religion.

If people like Edmund Wilson had read a story of this sort, I think Edmund Wilson and the others would have gone slower in finding malignity in the governess.

There is a phrase, "I'll be damned if I'll accept it." People say it, and they all have something that Miles and Richard Digby had, though we don't think the persons trying to tell people what they'll be damned if they'll accept, are necessarily bad. But a state of acute indecision can make, as I said, for extinction.

The Hawthorne story is one of the many vindications of the troubled and confused but essentially likable governess. She did not kill Miles. It was original sin in a high state—a high state of indecision, disruption, and persistence—that killed him.

Going now to Section 24. The governess has just asked Miles, in a very careful prose, if he took her letter—with lots of commas. Though it has been put so decorously and with such verbal finesse, things are happening.

My sense of how he received this suffered for a minute from something that I can describe only as a fierce split of my attention—a stroke that at first, as I sprang straight up, reduced me to the mere blind movement of getting hold of him, drawing him close, and, while I just fell for support against the nearest piece of furniture, instinctively keeping him with his back to the window.

This sentence is a pretty strong exemplification of the fact that the governess wanted to conquer reticence and say things, but that as she said things, she was afraid of her own words. Though the governess says this in her measured way, she is in a state of agitation and sharp wobble. She wants to get hold of Miles, and she falls against the furniture. She feels that the "presence" is around and Miles is aware of it.

The governess feels that at this time, because Miles has to make up his mind, he may try to get out of it by going back to business as usual. Peter Quint knows that (he's in the business), and so he is going to be around. This is a showdown. The governess is not perfect; hardly. Yet the governess is someone who is shouting a little for the dawn. She is a precursor; she is a little like Columbus. He discovered America and never knew he did: he thought it was India. So it seems that if we can forgive Columbus, we should forgive the governess. We build better than we know, as Wordsworth said.

The appearance was full upon us that I had already had to deal with here: Peter Quint had come into view like a sentinel before a prison. The next thing I saw was that, from outside, he had reached the window, and then I knew that, close to the glass and glaring in through it, he offered once more to the room his white face of damnation.

As the governess is critical of herself, she still uses these theological terms. "His white face of damnation" is a strong term.

It represents but grossly what took place within me at the sight to say that on the second my decision was made; yet I believe that no woman so overwhelmed ever in so short a time recovered her grasp of the *act*.

She says the decision is so final, so utter, but one can say perhaps it wasn't. If one were rewriting the story in the manner of, let us say, John Bunyan, one could have something like this: "Miles, you are now strong enough to meet your tempter. There is Peter Quint outside! Look at him and look at me! Do I stand for something you want more than that being there? I know that I do, and I know that it is easy now for you to decide." And Miles would say, "I prefer you to him." But what the governess does is to keep Miles away from Peter Quint.

The other way would be very glorious. The story could end that way, and perhaps Peter Quint would vanish with a great hiss. Such things have been. St. Anthony would always send the devils away with a hiss, though he suffered a great deal.

But the governess uses the protective way: "Oh, come to me—and I don't want you to see Peter Quint!" She thinks that is a complete decision, and never did a woman "so overwhelmed ever in so short a time" recover "her grasp of the *act*." I could doubt this a little.

It came to me in the very horror of the immediate presence that the act would be, seeing and facing what I saw and faced, to keep the boy himself unaware.

I think she is a little wrong here. This is a mistake of what is called technique, but her heart is in the right place.

The inspiration—I can call it by no other name—was
that I felt how voluntarily, how transcendently, I *might*.
It was like fighting with a demon for a human soul, and
when I had fairly so appraised it I saw how the human
soul—held out, in the tremor of my hands, at arm's
length—had a perfect dew of sweat on a lovely childish
forehead.

So the governess is aware of the tribulation of Miles.
He has sweat on his "lovely childish forehead"; and she
does, as women have very often tried to do, shelter him.
It doesn't work. We must surmise that the governess
made a mistake.

The face that was close to mine was as white as the face
against the glass, and out of it presently came a sound,
not low nor weak, but as if from much further away, that
I drank like a waft of fragrance.
"Yes—I took it."

Now when the governess has succeeded in eliciting a
confession from Miles about the letter, she gets too
pleased with herself, and she has too much joy. Instead
of saying, "Well, this is part of the story; it is very good
indeed," she enfolds him to herself. This enfolding shows
that she wanted to be on his side; she wanted to be too
much on his side. This is what is called "Being against
evil while still wanting to coddle it when it appears
good." Many mothers have made the same mistake.

At this, with a moan of joy, I enfolded, I drew him
close; and while I held him to my breast, where I could
feel in the sudden fever of his little body, the tremendous
pulse of his little heart, I kept my eyes on the thing at the
window and saw it move and shift its posture.

She is using two means. On the one hand she wants to show Miles that this thing doesn't stand for him. On the other, she wants to use the logic of hugging. The two get mixed up. "Don't you think that 3 and 4 make 7, dear? she asked, as she gave him a big hug."

The next sentence brings up something important in James: the idea of the beast in the jungle. I talked earlier about the story with that title. The beast in the jungle represents James's idea of something always in us, hidden most of the time, but ready to jump out and take things. The governess is describing Quint outside the window:

> I have likened it to a sentinel, but its slow wheel, for a moment, was rather the prowl of a baffled beast.

We can get the idea that Quint represents the desire in Miles or anybody to take over things and do it secretly. Of course, Quint has that in himself.

Then the governess gets too sure of herself. Just because she has got Miles to say that he took the letter, she feels virtue has won over the whole front, which it hasn't.

> It was the very confidence that I might now defy him, as well as the positive certitude, by this time, of the child's unconsciousness, that made me go on.
> "What did you take it for?"
> "To see what you said about me."

This is very direct.

> "You opened the letter?"
> "I opened it."

No fancy stuff here. Miles has been interested in just how much the governess knew and what she was telling the uncle.

> My eyes were now, as I held him off a little again, on Miles's own face, in which the collapse of mockery showed me how complete was the ravage of uneasiness.

The governess has been quite easily admitting that she was enfolding Miles, taking him to herself; but then the other, the more critical governess is also present, and this governess is keen. The fact that both things are stated shows that the governess wants to tell the whole truth. She wants to show herself as impulsively maternal, but also as having good judgment. This is the way mothers are. There is the silly department and the critical department: all mothers have both.

Because there is a "ravage of uneasiness," she gathers that there is a "collapse of mockery." This shows that the governess had seen Miles as a mocking person, a scornful person, a contemptuous person; and she can remember that, though right now she is hugging the little darling to her.

> And what did this strain of trouble matter when my eyes went back to the window only to see that the air was clear and — by my personal triumph — the influence quenched?

The governess then is too anxious; she is too ready to say the thing is all clear. This is like many people: "We've now had a reconciliation and from now on, it will never happen again." It is a big mistake. It likely will happen again. And yet that doesn't mean that the drift of before was wrong. It simply means that evil is like an apartment house and may have a thousand rooms.

So the governess gets too elated and she is too ready to be reconciled. People are. "This won't happen again, will it, dear? Now we'll be O.K." The governess feels that heaven has come:

> There was nothing there. I felt that the cause was mine and that I should surely get *all*.

There are a lot of italics around here. Then she says to Miles:

> "And you found nothing!"—I let my elation out.
> He gave the most mournful, thoughtful little headshake. "Nothing."
> "Nothing, nothing!" I almost shouted in my joy.

This is very silly, really.

> "Nothing, nothing," he sadly repeated.

This is a nice turn, however. She is just shouting in her joy and he is sadly repeating.

> I kissed his forehead; it was drenched. "So what have you done with it?"
> "I've burnt it."
> "Burnt it?" It was now or never. "Is that what you did at school?"
> Oh, what this brought up! "At school?"

And Miles is a little disappointed, because the idea of all he did being stealing and burning letters—well, it doesn't suit him.

"Did you know I mightn't go back?"

"I know everything."

He gave me at this the longest and strangest look. "Everything?"

"Everything. Therefore *did* you—? But I couldn't say it again.

Miles could, very simply. "No. I didn't steal."

If the governess was trying to put on a show, she would not put down her little failures. She felt Miles might steal, and then Miles tells her he didn't, and she believes him utterly.

My face must have shown him I believed him utterly; yet my hands—but it was for pure tenderness—shook him as if to ask him why, if it was all for nothing, he had condemned me to months of torment.

"What then did you do?"

She gets disturbed and shakes him. That is done a lot. Some things come clear and others don't, and it is all very annoying.

He looked in vague pain all round the top of the room and drew his breath, two or three times over, as if with difficulty. He might have been standing at the bottom of the sea and raising his eyes to some faint green twilight. "Well—I said things."

This drawing his breath two or three times over is a hint of what is going to happen: anxiety is shown in breathing hard.

Miles has some sense of very bad things, and he can't express it entirely, so he says, "Well—I said things." Miles is in the contempt business. He did take this letter, but stealing wasn't the most important activity. What he did likely do was to say things, to make fun of others, and to get people to make fun of others while he could make fun of them. In other words, he liked to see people in ludicrous situations. This may seem very funny, but it does have or can have a deep malignity to it.

I have seen children talk and gossip, and it stinks. But James couldn't talk about children that way: "It has in it the worst stench coming from the bottomless pit of a nauseating hell"—that is what he would like to have said about this way that children can talk about others, including adults. I have seen it. It is nauseating; it stinks; it comes from hell; it is the desire to have contempt. There are all kinds of imperialistic, oily twists that go on in children's conversations. James doesn't want to come out with it, because he was not in a position to denounce the budding evils of human buds. He didn't want to. I, not having his courtesy, come out with it. In *The Turn of the Screw*, all of this is very vague. We only know in the last chapter that Miles "says things." It has to do with the old idea of the devil as the bearer of evil tidings.

Miles says:

> "Well,—I said things."
> "Only that?"
> "They thought it was enough!"
> "To turn you out for?"

James doesn't describe things utterly, and we should ask why. I think James felt that if Miles said what things he told about others, which he wanted others to keep on telling—it might not have as much of an effect as if he didn't try to describe it at all.

Continuing, the governess asks:

"And these things came round—?"

"To the masters? Oh, yes!" he answered very simply. "But I didn't know they'd tell."

"The masters? They didn't—they've never told. That's why I ask you."

He turned to me again his little beautiful fevered face. "Yes, it was too bad."

"Too bad?"

"What I suppose I sometimes said. To write home."

The governess doesn't fully get this. She knows theologically that something is wrong. She knows an awful thing is going on. She wants to understand it. She wants to fight it. She can see Peter Quint and Miss Jessel representing evil, but as this profound evil takes form in detail, branches out into everyday doings, she can't follow it. It is too bad.

I can't name the exquisite pathos of the contradiction given to such a speech by such a speaker; I only know that the next instant I heard myself throw off with homely force: "Stuff and nonsense!" But the next after that I must have sounded stern enough. "What were these things?"

My sternness was all for his judge, his executioner; yet it made him avert himself again, and that movement made *me,* with a single bound and an irrepressible cry, spring straight upon him. For there again, against the glass, as if to blight his confession and stay his answer, was the hideous author of our woe—the white face of damnation.

Because Miles is disappointed with the incomplete seeing of the governess, he wrongly wants Quint again.

I felt a sick swim at the drop of my victory and all the return of my battle, so that the wildness of my veritable leap only served as a great betrayal.

The governess feels that once more she didn't give the perfect statement; but she is human. In the phrase "a great betrayal," there is something she feels she might not have done, and she would have been right in not doing it.

> I saw him, from the midst of my act, meet it with a divin- ation, and on the perception that even now he only guessed, and that the window was still to his own eyes free, I let the impulse flame up to convert the climax of his dismay into the very proof of his liberation. "No more, no more, no more!" I shrieked, as I tried to press him against me, to my visitant.

The way she takes has goodness of purpose, certainly; the detail, however, cannot be wholly praised. I don't think Miles liked that shrieking.

> "Is she *here?*" Miles panted as he caught with his sealed eyes the direction of my words. Then as his strange "she" staggered me and, with a gasp, I echoed it, "Miss Jessel, Miss Jessel!" he with a sudden fury gave me back.

Miles, I think, also could have contempt for Miss Jessel. He was one of those boys who had contempt for everybody coming his way. I think that as the governess here shows insufficiency, he gets an idea that if every- thing had worked right, he could have had contempt for her too.

> I seized, stupefied, his supposition—some sequel to what we had done to Flora, but this made me only want to show him that it was better still than that. "It's not Miss Jessel! But it's at the window—straight before us. It's *there*—the coward horror, there for the last time!"
> At this, after a second in which his head made the movement of a baffled dog's on a scent and then gave a

frantic little shake for air and light, he was at me in a white rage,

Miles, because he doesn't know what choice to make, has the anger of acute uncertainty.

bewildered, glaring vainly over the place and missing wholly, though it now, to my sense, filled the room like the taste of poison, the wide, overwhelming presence. "It's *he?*"

This means that even with all Miles's confusion, he cannot have Quint as he had him once. He has seen too much. He can't get back to the contempt, but he can't have something he can respect. He is caught between the contempt and respect, and it is a fearful thing.

I was so determined to have all my proof that I flashed into ice to challenge him. "Whom do you mean by he?"
"Peter Quint—you devil!" His face gave again, round the room, its convulsed supplication. "*Where?*"

The difficulty with Quint changes into a difficulty with the governess too, and Miles wants to curse everything in sight.

They are in my ears still, his supreme surrender of the name and his tribute to my devotion. "What does he matter now, my own?—what will he *ever* matter? *I* have you."

And the governess, strangely, gets placid. At least Miles said the name, and it means he did see Quint. We see the rigid criticism and then the desire to be maternal, bosomy; and the bad mingling confuses Miles.

I launched at the beast, "but he has lost you for ever!"

And then, because she gets too solicitous and trium-
phant, Miles is displeased. The governess is not prepared
for this great scene, just as Hamlet wasn't prepared for
everything.

> Then for the demonstration of my work, "There, *there!*"
> I said to Miles.
> But he had already jerked straight round, stared, glared
> again, and seen but the quiet day.

He couldn't get back to the old triumph.

> With the stroke of the loss I was so proud of he uttered
> the cry of a creature hurled over an abyss, and the gasp
> with which I recovered him might have been that of
> catching him in his fall.

The sense of loss and the sense that he cannot take what
he sees, is too much for him.

> I caught him, yes, I held him—it may be imagined with
> what a passion; but at the end of a minute I began to feel
> what it truly was that I held.

James is critizing the governess. There was a bad
mingling of opposites: the seeing and the motherly con-
soling.

> We were alone with the quiet day, and his little heart,
> dispossessed, had stopped.

Because of this indecision, Miles gets what can be
called a quiet tantrum. It is a little bit like what happens when babies turn blue with indecision: frantic
indecision.

But to show that the whole meaning was intended to be good, I refer you again to the Hawthorne passage where something similar happens to Richard Digby who, because he cannot accept something which somewhere he knows to be true, dies.

And so *The Turn of the Screw* ends with the awareness of evil but not the full conquering of it, and not the full love of what is different.

Epilogue, 1967

I. GENERAL OBSERVATIONS ON JAMES'S PROPAGANDA AS TECHNIQUE

The original meaning of propaganda, as anyone can see not wholly apart from Latin, is the sowing of seed. A novelist sows seed; Henry James sows seed. We, as ground, are pleased.

What seed then does the sower of *What Maisie Knew* and *The Turn of the Screw* sow?

It is seed asking us to participate more in the lives of others. It is seed asking us to know that other things feel and that the feelings of others are things which we diminish or are not interested in at a loss to ourselves. Insensitivity was seen by the author of *The Ambassadors* as a hazard.

Suppose we use Morton Dauwen Zabel in the introduction to his *Portable Henry James*, 1951. Zabel has James saying in a letter to Grace Norton of 1883:

> We never cease to feel, and though at moments we appear to, try to, pray to, there is something that holds one in one's place, makes it a standpoint in the universe which it is probably good not to forsake. (*Portable James*, p. 26.)

And Zabel presents this from an 1874 consideration of Turgenev:

We can welcome experience as it comes, and give it what it demands, in exchange for something which it is idle to pause to call much or little so long as it contributes to swell the volume of consciousness. In this there is mingled pain and delight, but over the mysterious mixture there hovers a visible rule, that bids us learn to will and seek to understand. (*Portable James,* p. 27.)

Why do I call this propaganda? What has it to do with James's technique? Why can it usefully be made equivalent to technique?

Well, there is a relation between what is called the "conscience of the artist" and the conscience of the pastor, or the conscience of the bank teller in a village. Conscience and technique are not unacquainted.

James as propagandist says in the two passages I have quoted that we have a perceptual obligation to the universe and a perceptual obligation to the feelings of a conscious being. He says this often. What he says is of him, him.

In the talks of 1953 on *The Turn of the Screw,* I presented Miles and Flora as using their minds to possess two not wholly solid, not wholly alive beings, out to possess them.

Through continuing their contemptuous conquest of the beings of Jessel and Quint, Miles and Flora showed their way of seeing the world.

It is just the way James does not have in his technique. Instead of capturing a person through his feeling, James was hoping that the full existence of another person would bring his—James's—life and feeling to graceful fulness.

The technique of James is to see a feeling in every way possible and present it so.

The technique of Miles and Flora is to possess another —and certainly, seem to be possessed—and so have a nonartistic victory over what James calls in the Norton quotation, the "something that holds one in one's place, makes it a standpoint in the universe"; and in the Turgenev quotation, the "visible rule" that "hovers over" the "mysterious mixture" that "bids us learn to will and seek to understand."

The language in the Turgenev quotation is, as can be seen, much like the language, roaming between the touchable and the invisible, which we find in *The Turn of the Screw*.

James says in *The Turn of the Screw* that the children were not going by the "visible rule." Nor were Quint and Jessel. And there have been others who did not care much for this hovering "visible rule."

And what about the world we walk about in and have impressions of so much?

II. *THE TURN OF THE SCREW* IS THE WORLD GOING ABOUT

There was, then, in Henry James some sight of how a person—a world going about—should see other persons and the world itself—which, like an individual, is going about something.

As a person goes about his business, which, usually, he knows very little, he can welcome evil as a means of accomplishing that business. The business, in terms of a person, can be described as feeling as pleased as possible and as impressive as possible.

Most often a person, in order to be pleased, lies. Flora and Miles lie. Here they are like the diplomats who at various times have helped to cause war, or at least have not done enough to stop war. It is necessary to say that what was in the minds of two English children born in the second half of the 19th century was like what was in the minds of Sazonov, Delcassé, Bethmann-Hollweg, Grey—diplomats not wholly against lying and owning people. Evil often begins delicately and culminates massively.

James in being against the lying of the two children was against lying anywhere and by whomever. Lying is a big thing in history.

The children have tried to own their servants, Quint and Jessel, and the servants have tried to own them. The four have rather succeeded. In "Brooksmith," a servant includes his master within himself. And the story, with some meaning, ends this way:

> But the dim ghost of poor Brooksmith is one of those that I see. He had indeed been spoiled.

A ghost, with Henry James, is a feeling towards another that has become so much of yourself, it takes an outward form. The best illustration of this is in how Mrs. Marsden explains the existence of Sir Edmund Orme as ghost in a story which preceded *The Turn of the Screw* by a few years:

> It isn't what you say that makes the difference; it's what you feel.

In the story, "Sir Edmund Orme," the ghost exists for Mrs. Marsden because of how she felt towards Sir Edmund himself.

An aspect of the propaganda of Henry James is that our feelings about other people are as real as people themselves. Particularly, if we desire to make another person a submissive, lessened province of ourselves, may our feeling seem to stand and walk and visually be in space.

There is a relation between the willed evocation of Helen by Faustus in Marlowe's play and the dimmer evocation of Quint and Jessel by Miles and Flora.

Much in the work of Henry James comments on that high point of his perceptive, imaginative, and ethical life, *The Turn of the Screw*. "The Liar," for instance, of 1888 has two people in it, a good deal like Miles and Flora. The lying Colonel Capadose is like the boy; the sister is like the wife of the Colonel who affects her much, because, owning him, she'd rather that he be admirable and congenial than otherwise. The story ends somewhat as *The Turn of the Screw* ends.

The unseen and the seen are in James in an aesthetic relation. The unseen and seen when truly one are as lovely as anything; but when a person uses his imagination to own, to lessen others, the seen and unseen are put in a relation which, however interesting—evil is decidedly interesting—is ugly.

One of these days the dislike Marx had for the ownership of factories privately will be seen like James's distaste for the way people can own people. The feelings we don't see—here like ghosts in their partial reality (James has the phrase *Partial Portraits* as title of a book) —can be used unjustly by us as to other people. James was always working to see the meaning of a person's feeling to others. *The Sacred Fount* of 1901 is an ungainly attempt at showing how people incorporate other people into themselves, or organically acquire them, or something like this. The best way of putting it is that the American, Henry James, could be like the Swede, August Strindberg, in decrying emotion as acquisitive; not beautifully, courageously just.

Propaganda, surely, is not absent from what has been said. The South exploited Negroes; Victorian England, manufacturing Victorian England, exploited children. James is in the field of Karl Marx when Marx says men use machines to exploit other men; and in the field of Elizabeth Barrett Browning when, in "The Cry of the Children," the English poet says children are exploited by manufacturers of Great Britain.

Does James say that Miles and Flora contemptuously make use of Quint and Jessel, with these wishing to do well in the field of contempt, too? In the letter to Grace Norton quoted earlier, James asks for something other than contempt in the way we see people.

The biggest unearthly or, if one wishes, unseen objective of the human mind left to itself is contempt. Contempt is the main ugly thing in exploitation.

Contempt, while ugly, can work with ever so delicate, even vaporous material.

The work of Henry James — his propaganda — is to show how the complexities and powers of one mind, or several minds, could be active in behalf of a universe, large: and the same as and different from one person; and how the complexities and powers of a mind or minds could be used to narrow, selectively own, exploit, and have contempt for the outside world, or universe.

To make the world less is evil. To make for a quarrel between the oneness of the world and division in it is evil.

Evil, like matter, begins with the not seen, the ever so tenuous.

Propaganda, as technique, is present in the third part of this Epilogue, the Epilogue as Poems.

III. NOTATIONS, IN VERSE, ON THE NOVELISTIC
MANNER OF HENRY JAMES, 1843-1916

1. *There Are Non-Goings On*

Henry James
Is distinguished
By his great
Non-goings on.

2. *A Happening Is Completed by Observation*

What is observed is what happens in H. J.;
In other authors it is just what happens.

3. *Sometimes It Is Kind to Watch a Person Watching*

H. J. is kind enough
To watch a person watching;
He is not stodgily there, Oh Minerva!

4. *How Much Is the Soul an Adverb?*

With other authors
The soul is a noun;
Or a fable or a violent verb;
With H. J., the soul
Is an adverb.

5. *Parenthesis*

The greatest desire of the unconscious,
According to H. J.,
Is to be delicate;
There is delicate sweeping
And delicate penetration.

6. *Happening and Being*

Happening in H. J.
Is muted
To polite, surprising Being.

7. *James's Novels*

James's novels
Are a victory
Of fingertips
Over claws.

8. *Henry James Looks at Virtue*

Virtue, with H. J.,
Is comfort arising
From unimpeded awareness.

9. *It Is Kind for Us to Be Aware of Others'
Awareness*

According to H. J.,
The awareness of another possible awareness
Is the kindest deed ever.

10. *To Be Observed Is Not a Misfortune*

H. J. sees that person as fortunate
Who is unceasingly, indefinitely observed.

11. *A Thing Denuded of the Ways It
Can Be Seen Is Low*

A thing without its aspects
Is vulgar,
According to H. J.

12. *Definition Is Not Bleak*

> Definition is aroma
> With H. J.

13. *Time Has This Use*

> The purpose of Time,
> According to H. J.,
> Is to make observation possible.

14. *Space Defended as Purposeful*

> Space exists, according to H. J.,
> So that people have somewhere to be
> While they think of themselves
> Or others.

15. *Love Is Erudite Yearning*

> Love, according to H. J.,
> Is erudite sensitivity yearning
> For erudite sensitivity.

16. *Raison d'être for Colons*

> A colon exists for H. J.
> To mark a rather unexpected fluctuation
> Of a heart entangled
> In dim awareness.

17. *Rapidity Spoils Essence*

> According to H. J.,
> It should take years to say
> You like somebody;
> Otherwise you are impetuous.

18. *A Ghost*

A ghost
Is that part of your feeling
You don't see;
It looks to exist, your ghost,
Like a tree established,
A professor established.

19. *Heroic Quality of the Implicit*

The implicit
Is hero and
Heroine, in H. J.

20. *What the Greatest Event Is*

The greatest Event
In H. J.
Is the acquisition
Of new information.

21. *A Ghost Once More*

A ghost with H. J.
Is what we shouldn't have been
Or what we wanted to be—
A feeling, of course,
That can roam visibly near masonry
Or look at you across a well-made round table.

22. *A Smile Is Not Just for Simple Folk*

A smile with H. J.
Is as complex as the battle
Of Waterloo with Victor Hugo.

23. *A Gentleman's Knowledge Is Never Adequate about Anyone*

A gentleman, according to H. J.,
Is someone who doesn't assume
He is wholly informed
About anybody.

24. *The Heart, Yes*

The heart
With H. J.
Is a beating landscape.

25. *Possibility Visits*

Possibility sits at
The tables
In H. J.'s novels.

26. *Our Names: Downfall and Goal*

People try
To live
Up to their names
In H. J.'s novels.

27. *Forms Participate*

Forms shake hands
And invite each other to tea
In H. J.'s novels;
The tea is a means
Of the forms'
Taking on more solidity.

28. *Conversation Can Confirm Existence*

>   Conversation of people in H. J.
>   Is a means they have
>   Of deciding more
>   That they exist.

29. *What Is Not a Beginning?*

>   Even when something happens,
>   It seems
>   As if it were only
>   Beginning to happen.

30. *Falling Petals May Reveal the Flower*

>   As petals fall
>   In the guarded pages
>   Of the American novelist,
>   Now present,
>   The flower of fictional intent
>   May be better seen.

BOOKS QUOTED

Part 1
1. William Blake, *Poetical Works*, ed. John Sampson (Oxford: Oxford University Press, 1914), p. 100.
2. Henry Vaughan, *The Works of Henry Vaughan*, ed. L. C. Martin (Oxford: Clarendon Press, 1957), p. 419.
3. Henry James, *What Maisie Knew* (New York: Charles Scribner's Sons, 1923).
4. James, "Maud-Evelyn," *The Ghostly Tales of Henry James*, ed. Leon Edel (New Brunswick: Rutgers University Press, 1948).
5. James, "The Pupil," *The Novels and Tales of Henry James*, XI (New York: Charles Scribner's Sons, 1908).

Part 2
1. E. F. Benson, *As We Were* (London: Longmans, Green & Co., 1930), pp. 279-81, *passim*.
2. Edel, ed., *The Ghostly Tales*, p. 432.
3. James, *The Notebooks of Henry James*, ed. F. O. Matthiessen and Kenneth B. Murdock (New York: Oxford University Press, 1947), p. 178.
4. James, *The Turn of the Screw*, in *The Story: A Critical Anthology*, ed. Mark Schorer (New York: Prentice-Hall, Inc., 1950). Siegel used this edition because (as he says, pp. 35-36) it includes "Remarks from a Preface," by James; selections from Edmund Wilson's "The Ambiguity of Henry James"; and Robert Heilman's *"The Turn of the Screw* as Poem."—Ed.

Part 4
Nathaniel Hawthorne, "The Man of Adamant," *The Snow-Image and Other Twice-Told Tales*, Vol. III of *The Complete Works of Nathaniel Hawthorne* (Boston and New York: Houghton Mifflin Company, 1883).

Epilogue
1. James, *The Portable Henry James*, ed. Morton Dauwen Zabel (New York: The Viking Press, 1951), pp. 26, 27.
2. James, "Brooksmith," *The Lesson of the Master* (New York: Macmillan, 1891).
3. James, "Sir Edmund Orme," *The Ghostly Tales*.